THE WRITER'S TOOLBOX

The Writer's Toolbox

Using Rhetorical Devices to Improve Communication

by Patricia Samuelsen
with Meagan Samuelsen

SWEETWATER PUBLISHING

Patricia Samuelsen with Meagan Samuelsen
The Writer's Toolbox: Using Rhetorical Devices to Improve Communication

ISBN: 978-0-9846351-0-8

© 2011 by Patricia Samuelsen. All Rights Reserved.
  2013 Second Printing
  2018 Third Printing

Sweetwater Publishing
3110 Winchester Way, Sugar Land, TX 77479
281-980-5060
www.writerstoolbox.net

Cover image by Kimberly McMillen.

Unless otherwise indicated, all Scripture quotations are from The Holy Bible, English Standard Version, copyright (c) 2001 by Crossway Bibles, a division of Good News Publishers. Used by permission. All rights reserved.

All Rights Reserved. No portion of this book may be reproduced or transmitted in any form or by any means, electronic or mechanical, including photocopy, recording, or by an information storage and retrieval system without prior written permission of the publisher. Permission is granted for brief quotations in critical articles or reviews, provided that the authors' names and address are clearly cited.

Contents

Preface vii
Introduction 1

Devices of Association

Lesson 1: Simile 5
Lesson 2: Metaphor 11
Lesson 3: Personification 17
Lesson 4: Allusion 21
Lesson 5: Metonymy 25
Lesson 6: Synecdoche 29
Lesson 7: Review 35

Devices of Emphasis

Lesson 8: Climax 41
Lesson 9: Asyndeton 45
Lesson 10: Polysyndeton 49
Lesson 11: Irony 53
Lesson 12: Understatement 57
Lesson 13: Litotes 61
Lesson 14: Hyperbole 65
Lesson 15: Review 69

Devices of Balance & Restatement

Lesson 16: Parallelism — 75
Lesson 17: Chiasmus — 79
Lesson 18: Antithesis — 83
Lesson 19: Anaphora — 87
Lesson 20: Epistrophe — 91
Lesson 21: Anadiplosis — 95
Lesson 22: Epanalepsis — 99
Lesson 23: Review — 103

Devices of Decoration & Variety

Lesson 24: Ellipsis — 109
Lesson 25: Erotema — 113
Lesson 26: Alliteration — 117
Lesson 27: Assonance — 121
Lesson 28: Oxymoron — 125
Lesson 29: Onomatopoeia — 129
Lesson 30: Review — 133

Appendices

Appendix A: Rhetorical Devices in Context — 139
Appendix B: Review Games — 141
Appendix C: Definitions — 143
Appendix D: Answer Key — 147

Preface

Rhetoric is ubiquitous. We all experience and use it everyday–when we watch a commercial, when we write an essay, even when we converse around the dinner table. Rhetoric is simply the art of effective or persuasive speaking or writing. Over its 2500-year history, the study of style (especially the use of the devices we study in this book) has been an integral component of the study of rhetoric. We can let the academics decide whether rhetorical devices are necessary to the thinking process or simply serve as added ornamentation, but speakers and writers for thousands of years have agreed that these tools give clarity and beauty to our communication.

The Writer's Toolbox focuses on the use of rhetorical devices. While not a complete writing curriculum, *The Writer's Toolbox* helps you understand, recognize, and practice some valuable tools of clear and effective communication. Rich in examples from famous authors and orators, this book can act as an unintimidating introduction to the rhythms of well-crafted writing. We want you to understand that words matter, and that using words skillfully is one of the joys of life.

The Writer's Toolbox is a great addition to any writing, public speaking, or debating program, and can be used in a classroom setting or at home. Anyone interested in the ways words work will enjoy these lessons and examples from literature and oratory. Whether you are fifteen or fifty, *The Writer's Toolbox* helps you improve your writing without a large time commitment. Each lesson takes no more than 30 minutes to complete, and you can easily finish the book in a school year by completing one lesson every week. For use in the classroom, we have included a few group review games in the appendices.

This book was written for (and with the help of) the 2009/2010 Primer students in The Great Conversation class at Schola, a meeting place for teachers and pupils, in Sugar Land, Texas. Without these special students and their enthusiasm for the "writing magic" in rhetorical devices, we would never have made it past the first lesson! Thanks to Marcella, Maria, Michela, Faith, Anna, Hannah, Rachel, Andrew, Chris, Susanna, James, Dylan, and Tim for their excitement and encouragement. Many thanks to Meagan for bringing her own insights and "writing magic" to this endeavor, to Amanda for her careful eye for detail, and to Zing and Cathy for a final polishing. Any errors are my own.

—Patricia Samuelsen
August, 2010

INTRODUCTION

Over 2500 years ago, the Greek philosopher Aristotle wrote *The Art of Rhetoric*, in which he discussed various aspects of communication as it was practiced by the great orators of his day. The first two sections of his work concentrated on the invention and arrangement of an argument. In the last section he delved into style, including a discussion of what we call rhetorical devices.

So, what are rhetorical devices? Well, let's compare the process of writing to the process of building a house.[1] Let's say that you already have your blueprint, your overall structure. In writing, we might call that an outline. Let's also say that you have your materials at hand. For us that means the supports for your argument—or, perhaps, the plot elements of the Great American Novel you have in your head! Now you are ready to do the heavy construction work. But how? How will you bring your material and your design together?[2]

This is when you need some tools–a hammer and some nails, an axe, a chisel or two.[3] In your writing, rhetorical devices are your tools.[4] They help you work the details: the order of your words, the use of conjunctions, the rhythm of each individual phrase.[5] They allow you to craft your writing on a micro-level, sentence by sentence, manipulating your materials to fit into your larger plan.

---

1   Simile
2   Rhetorical Question
3   Asyndeton
4   Metaphor
5   Asyndeton

It is useful to note that everyone uses rhetorical devices in speech and writing. They are an integral part of everyday communication, some of them so common that we may miss them. But, like the tools in your grandfather's workshop, they can be used clumsily and without knowledge, or skillfully with an understanding of their power.[6] Knowledge of your rhetorical tools will make your writing structurally sound and beautiful.

The goal of this book is three-fold: to help you identify, appreciate, and use rhetorical devices. Every lesson begins with a simple explanation of one of the rhetorical devices along with examples from literature, oratory, and real life. The lesson closes with suggestions for the best way to begin using the device. After each lesson are exercises where you can try out the tool for yourself. The answers for the exercises are at the back of the book along with some useful appendices.

Be sure to continue reviewing the devices you've already studied in order to master their definitions and uses. Look for examples of the devices in literature, newspapers, comics, commercials, billboards.[7] Each time you recognize a rhetorical device, you will better understand the tools at your disposal.

These tools are as old as the lever, as powerful as the hammer, and as sensitive to the touch of the craftsman as the chisel and lathe.[8] The only way to learn how to use a tool is to practice. So, what are you waiting for?[9] Open the toolbox, try out each device, see what it does best.[10] You'll become an expert craftsman of sentences and paragraphs, a master builder of ideas.[11]

---

6   Antithesis
7   Asyndeton
8   Parallelism
9   Rhetorical Question
10 Asyndeton
11 Metaphor

1
DEVICES OF ASSOCIATION

LESSON 1

Oliver had fallen behind on his algebra homework. Now polynomial factoring loomed over his weekend like a dark cloud threatening to spoil the fun.

Wait a minute. What does a dark cloud have to do with algebra homework? It's true that algebra and clouds are two unlike things, but they do have at least one thing in common: they can both spoil a fun weekend as quickly as a list of Saturday chores from your mother.

Welcome to the world of similes. When you compare two unlike things, you use the characteristics of one to help you describe the other. The resulting word picture is more vivid and interesting than a simple description.

One of the most familiar similes is by the poet Robert Burns:

My love is like a red, red rose
That's newly sprung in June.

When Burns says that the girl he loves is like a red rose, he doesn't mean that she has thorns or roots or needs to be watered. He might mean that she is young and beautiful. He might even mean that she smells nice. That's part of the fun of similes. When you read a simile, you have to figure out which characteristics are being transferred from one subject to the other.

Similes have primary and secondary subjects. The primary subject is the thing that the poet is actually talking about (in this case, "my love"). The secondary subject is the thing to which the poet is comparing the primary subject ("a red, red rose").

simile

SIM-uh-lee

From Latin
similis "a like thing"

An explicit comparison of two unlike things, often employing "like" or "as."

Most similes use the comparative words "like" and "as" to compare their primary and secondary subjects. Look at these examples:

Mint ice cream is like a cool breeze on a hot day.

He swims as fast as a fish.

Other similes (the sneaky ones!) do not use "like" or "as." In the following examples, for instance, the comparative word is an adjective.

His speech was smoother than butter...
—Psalm 55:21 (NASV)

"I'm happier than a tornado in a trailer park."
—Tow Mater, *Cars*

Sometimes, it might not be clear to us what the objects being compared have in common. Then the comparison can be elaborated, as you can see in the following examples:

And money is like muck, not good except it be spread.
—Francis Bacon

Life is like an onion:
You peel it off one layer at a time, and sometimes you weep.
—Carl Sandburg

Use similes to emphasize a certain characteristic of the thing being described. When you use a simile, your reader or listener can form a mental picture of the comparison, helping them understand what you're trying to communicate. Similes help you to think carefully about your subject and add spice to your writing.

I. Appreciating Similes

A. Explain the following examples of simile.

1. "I feel thin . . . like butter scraped over too much bread."
   — Bilbo Baggins in J.R.R. Tolkien, *The Hobbit*

   a. What is being described?

   b. What is it being compared to?

   c. How are the two subjects alike?

2. "The kingdom of heaven is like treasure hidden in a field, which a man found and covered up. Then in his joy he goes and sells all that he has and buys that field."
   — Matthew 13:44

   a. What is being described?

   b. What is it being compared to?

   c. How are the two subjects alike?

3. How like the winter hath my absence been.
   — William Shakespeare, "Sonnet 97"

   a. What is being described?

   b. What is it being compared to?

   c. How are the two subjects alike?

4. In the light of a king's face there is life,
   and his favor is like the clouds that bring the spring rain.

   — Proverbs 16:15

   a. What is being described?

   b. What is it being compared to?

   c. How are the two subjects alike?

5. He clasps the crag with crooked hands;
   Close to the sun in lonely lands,
   Ringed with the azure world, he stands.

   The wrinkled sea beneath him crawls;
   He watches from his mountain walls,
   And like a thunderbolt he falls.

   — Alfred, Lord Tennyson, "The Eagle"

   a. What is being described?

   b. What is it being compared to?

   c. How are the two subjects alike?

6.   From the camp
   the troops were turning out now, thick as bees
   that issue from some crevice in a rock face,
   endlessly pouring forth, to make a cluster
   and swarm on blooms of summer here and there,
   glinting and droning, busy in bright air.

   — Homer, *The Iliad*, trans. Robert Fitzgerald, Book 2, Lines 98-103

   a. What is being described?

   b. What is it being compared to?

   c. How are the two subjects alike?

II. Writing Similes

A. Write similes by completing the following sentences. Many similes are clichés (phrases that are overused and show a lack of original thought). Try to write original similes that are fresh and interesting. Think about what part of the primary subject you want to emphasize. Then think of something that is "like" that.

1. Her smile is like _____ .

2. The library is like _____ .

3. _____ is like a volcano.

4. _____ is like a bubbling brook.

5. He eats like _____ .

6. These cookies taste like _____ .

7. The celebration was as _____ as _____ .

8. The sun was as _____ as _____ .

B. Write your own similes.

1. You have a huge dog. Use a simile to describe how huge.

2. You've done a great job cleaning up your room. Use a simile to describe how it looks now.

3. You've been working on your math homework for six hours already. Use a simile to show how worn out you are feeling.

4. You're spending a whole week with your favorite cousins at the beach. Use a simile to show how you feel about it.

LESSON 2

metaphor

MET-uh-for

From Greek
meta "over, across"
pherein "to carry, bear"

An implied comparison made by referring to one thing as another.

Although she was nervous at the beginning of the gymnastics competition, Charlotte's performance was a rare gem, and she returned home proudly flashing a gold medal.

Charlotte's performance certainly wasn't a stone, but the beauty and value of a gem tell us that Charlotte's routine was outstanding. Like a simile, a metaphor uses certain characteristics of one thing to help describe the other. Unlike a simile, however, a metaphor doesn't say that something is *like* something else, it says that it *is* something else.

Some metaphors are clearly stated:

At the family reunion Mary was a mother hen gathering her brood under her wings.

Others might be harder to spot. These are called implied metaphors because they imply but do not spell out the comparison, like this example:

Mary clucked her concern.

In this example, Mary is not explicitly identified as a mother hen, but her nurturing characteristics are implied by a verb that makes us think of a mother hen.

Sometimes, like a simile, a metaphor must spell out the similarity between the subjects:

"I am the good shepherd. The good shepherd lays down his life for the sheep."
—John 10:11

In this New Testament metaphor, Jesus explains that, like a good shepherd, he is willing to die for his flock of followers.

Like a simile, a metaphor has two subjects. Attributes are borrowed from the secondary subject (in the example above, the good shepherd) and given to the primary subject (Jesus).

Be sure to keep metaphors consistent or you will end up with a "mixed metaphor" like the one in this example:

He threw a cold shoulder on that idea.

This mixed metaphor combines two ideas that convey disapproval: the cold shoulder and cold water. Either would work, but you can't throw a cold shoulder!

Sometimes metaphors are called abbreviated similes. Like similes they liven up ordinary language and help us think about familiar subjects in new and different ways. A metaphor is even more powerful than a simile, however, because it actually equates two things in our imagination.

Metaphors are one of the writer's and poet's most important tools. They call up vivid images and memorable connections for the reader without using a lot of words. They help make abstract concepts concrete and make descriptions more interesting and powerful.

Use metaphors to startle your reader into understanding. A fresh metaphor helps your reader to think differently about your topic. It connects two seemingly unrelated ideas to reveal a surprising truth.

I. Appreciating Metaphor

A. Explain the following examples of metaphor.

1. "I am the vine; you are the branches."

   —John 15:5a

   a. What is being described?

   b. What is it being compared to?

   c. How are the two subjects alike?

2. The fog comes
   on little cat feet.

   It sits looking
   over harbor and city
   on silent haunches
   and then moves on.

   —Carl Sandburg, "The Fog"

   a. What is being described?

   b. What is it being compared to?

   c. How are the two subjects alike?

3. We all walk on very thin ice. We all pretend we don't, but we know how easy it is for our present happiness to be shattered.

   —William Boyd

   a. What is being described?

   b. What is it being compared to?

   c. How are the two subjects alike?

4. "All the world's a stage,
   And all the men and women merely players;
   They have their exits and their entrances;
   And one man in his time plays many parts,
   His acts being seven ages."
   —Jaques in William Shakespeare, *As You Like It*, Act 2, Scene 7

   a. What is being described?

   b. What is it being compared to?

   c. How are the two subjects alike?

B. Explain these mixed metaphors.

1. He's burning the midnight oil from both ends.

   a. What is the first metaphor?

   b. What is the second metaphor?

   c. What do they mean?

2. He's a little green behind the ears.

   a. What is the first metaphor?

   b. What is the second metaphor?

   c. What do they mean?

Lesson 2: Metaphor | 15

II. Writing Metaphors

A. Write metaphors describing your own family. Using the category of tools, books, or musical instruments, write a metaphor for each person in your family. First, choose a category, then make a list of several examples of your category. Here are some examples to get you started. Add some more in the category you selected.

Tools	Books	Musical Instruments
hammer	dictionary	violin
wrench	thesaurus	trumpet
pliers	novel	flute
saw	poetry	xylophone
clamp	song book	drums

Think of characteristics that at least four family members have in common with various examples of your category. Turn that image into a metaphor, e.g. "In my family library, my young brother Ben is an encyclopedia–he always has the answer to any question."

1.

2.

3.

4.

B. Write metaphors by completing these sentences.

1. The first day of school is

2. Summer vacation is

3. A family vacation is

4. Hanging out with friends is

LESSON 3

As Oliver raced to finish his homework before leaving for school, the printer choked up and thwarted his best intentions.

personification

per-sahn-uh-fi-KAY-shun

Attributing human qualities to something that is not human.

Is the printer actually choking? Choking happens when you have something stuck in your throat. Does a printer have a throat? No, but when we say that the printer has choked, we bring to mind the experience of choking, perhaps the sound of coughing to clear one's throat or the idea of an obstruction in a small space. We have just made the printer a person by our words. Personification can be viewed as a special kind of metaphor that gives human characteristics to an animal, thing, or idea, as in these examples:

Love laughs at misfortune.

This coffee is strong enough to get up and walk away.

As human beings, we tend to view the world in human terms, so it's not surprising that we give human characteristics to inanimate objects or ideas in everyday life.

Giving familiar characteristics to unfamiliar things allows us to define and explain concepts in terms of everyday human experience and action. When we "humanize" animals, objects and ideas, we understand them better because we know what it's like to be human.

Authors and poets commonly use personification to bring the inanimate world to life for readers. When we read an effective personification, we use what we know about ourselves as humans to learn more about other aspects of the world. The poet Joyce Kilmer wrote a poem about trees, in which he gave trees several human characteristics. What human attributes do you notice in the poem?

> I think that I shall never see
> A poem lovely as a tree.
> A tree whose hungry mouth is pres't
> Against the sweet earth's flowing breast;
> A tree that looks at God all day,
> And lifts her leafy arms to pray;
> A tree that may in summer wear
> A nest of robins in her hair;
> Upon whose bosom snow has lain;
> Who intimately lives with rain.
> Poems are made by fools like me,
> But only God can make a tree.

Companies use personification to create memorable images of their products. Are you familiar with any of the following?

Mr. Clean® (a household cleaner)   **Chore Boy®** (a scouring pad)
Aunt Jemima® (syrup)   **Little Debbie®** (snack cakes)

Advertisers also personify products to encourage us to purchase them. Perhaps we identify more with a product that is personified with human characteristics we can relate to.

Oreo®: Milk's favorite cookie.

Use personification to help your reader picture abstract concepts. You can personify objects and ideas by using personal pronouns like *he* or *she* to refer to them. You can also describe them as having human emotions, appearance, or abilities.

Lesson 3: Personification | 19

I. Appreciating Personification

A. Explain the following examples of personification.

1. The plants were crying for my attention.

    a. What is being personified?

    b. What human characteristics are given to it?

2. Time will say nothing but I told you so.
    — W. H. Auden, "If I Could Tell You"

    a. What is being personified?

    b. What human characteristics are given to it?

3. When the waters saw you, O God,
   when the waters saw you, they were afraid;
   indeed, the deep trembled.
    — Psalm 77:16

    a. What is being personified?

    b. What human characteristics are given to it?

4. Death be not proud, though some have called thee
   Mighty and dreadful, for, thou art not so,
   For, those whom thou think'st, thou dost overthrow,
   Die not, poor death, nor yet canst thou kill me.
    — John Donne, "Holy Sonnet X"

    a. What is being personified?

    b. What human characteristics are given to it?

II. Writing Personifications

A. Create a personification by replacing the verb in parenthesis with a word that gives human characteristics to the subject.

1. The cursor (moves) across the computer screen.

2. The alarm clock (buzzes) in the early morning.

3. The sun (shines) on a hot day.

4. The stream (trickles) over the rocks.

5. The car (drives) down the icy road.

B. Choose five noun and verb pairs from the following lists, then expand each pair into a sentence by personifying the noun.

   Nouns: grass, waves, stars, computer, books, mountains, homework, campfire, trumpet, breakfast, boots, train, love

   Verbs: beckon(s), leap(s), smile(s), command(s), consider(s), gazes(s), laugh(s), joke(s), feast(s), scold(s), encourage(s), trip(s)

1. The pile of books commands me to attend to my studies.

2.

3.

4.

5.

LESSON 4

allusion

uh-LOO-zhun

From Latin
allusio "a playing with"

A short, informal reference to a famous person or event.

Note: Don't confuse the rhetorical device "allusion" with "illusion," a deceptive appearance or impression.

Oliver shrugged his heavy backpack onto his shoulders and trudged off to class, looking like Atlas himself.

This description of poor Oliver trudging off to class with his heavy backpack makes a short, informal reference to the mythological Titan who was condemned to hold the heavens on his shoulders. It conjures up a mental picture of the mighty Atlas bent beneath his heavy burden and conveys in one word something about Oliver and his backpack that is more vivid than simply saying the backpack is heavy.

Allusions may refer to either persons or events. They are most often drawn from the Bible, history, mythology, or literature, as in the following examples:

Like a prodigal son, he returned to his home and received a warm welcome.

This allusion assumes the reader is familiar with the story, found in Luke 15:11-32, of the son who demands his inheritance, wastes it in a far-off country, and contritely returns to his home, where he is welcomed with open arms by his father. Notice how the two words "prodigal son" convey a picture of someone expecting an angry reception but receiving instead a loving welcome.

Beware of Greeks bearing gifts.

This famous warning assumes familiarity with the story of the Greeks entering the city of Troy hidden in a "gift" of a large wooden horse. Once in the city, they climbed out of the horse and attacked the Trojans. This brief allusion reminds us that sometimes it is wise to "look a gift horse in the mouth."

If this tax increase is signed by the President, we can expect another tea party.

Since the fateful night of the Boston Tea Party, the term has been used as an allusion to a tax revolt. These words help us think of a group of citizens who are fed up with perceived injustice and ready to take matters into their own hands.

One special kind of allusion called an eponym substitutes the name of a person famous for a particular attribute in place of the attribute itself.

Every army fears the presence of a Benedict Arnold.

General Benedict Arnold betrayed the colonies during the American Revolution and switched sides to the British. Now Benedict Arnold is synonymous with a turncoat. Just the mention of his name conjures up a sense of betrayal.

Allusions act as a kind of shorthand communication among those with a shared body of knowledge. By now, you should have noticed that they only work if the reader is familiar with the same people and events as the writer. You can increase your understanding of allusions by wide reading in history, literature, and the Bible.

Although they must be used with care, allusions can convey clear pictures with just a few words. To use allusions successfully, you should choose references that will be familiar to your audience. Your peers may not be familiar with events from World War II, and your grandparents might not recognize an allusion to the latest pop star. Not only should the person or event be familiar to your audience, but it must also possess an attribute that conveys the meaning you intend to communicate. Don't mention the prodigal son if you're trying to convey a picture of a traitor.

I. Appreciating Allusion

A. Explain the following examples of allusion. You may need to look up the reference in order to understand the allusion.

1. "I violated the Noah rule: predicting rain doesn't count; building arks does."
   — Investor Warren Buffett

   a. What is the person or event being alluded to?

   b. What does the allusion illustrate?

2. My father's brother, but no more like my father
   Than I to Hercules.
   — Hamlet in William Shakespeare, *Hamlet*, Act 1, Scene 2

   a. What is the person or event being alluded to?

   b. What does the allusion illustrate?

3. The Scylla of plot and the Charybdis of total plotlessness.
   — Source Unknown

   a. What is the person or event being alluded to?

   b. What does the allusion illustrate?

4. I was as much affected by the faint hum of a mosquito making its invisible and unimaginable tour through my apartment at earliest dawn, ... as I could be by any trumpet that ever sang of fame. It was Homer's requiem; itself an *Iliad* and *Odyssey* in the air, singing its own wrath and wanderings.
   — Henry David Thoreau, *Walden*

   a. What is the person or event being alluded to?

   b. What does the allusion illustrate?

II. Writing Allusions

A. Write six sentences, each alluding to one of the following events or persons. You may need to look up the reference in order to understand the allusion.

    Scrooge   <u>Pollyanna</u>   Donnybrook
    Titanic (ship)   Mother Theresa Romeo and Juliet
    Jonah   Achilles' Heel   Pyrrhic victory
    Waterloo   Three Stooges   Rubicon

1. My mother's sunny disposition would put <u>Pollyanna</u> herself to shame.

2.

3.

4.

5.

6.

LESSON 5

metonymy

me-TON-uh-mee

From Greek
meta, "change"
onoma "name"

A reference to an object or concept by using a word closely related to or suggested by the original word.

"As soon as the kettle boils, I'll make you a cup of tea," Charlotte called to her ill mother.

Surely Charlotte knows that a tea kettle can't boil. She's referring to the water in the tea kettle, of course. Referring to an object by using a word closely related to it is called metonymy.

We use metonymy so commonly that we barely recognize it. Here are some examples:

The White House and Capitol Hill announced today that they will cooperate in drafting a health care plan.

"White House" refers to the executive branch of the government, while "Capitol Hill" refers to the legislative branch. Each branch is represented by the place where it works.

Detroit has continued to manufacture the cars that consumers, rather than the government, prefer.

In this common metonymy, we use the name of the city where many cars are manufactured to refer to the car manufacturers themselves.

Metonymy is also common in literature:

"Friends, Romans, countrymen, lend me your ears."
—Mark Antony in William Shakepeare, *Julius Caesar,* Act 3, Scene 2

Here, the word "ears" (the part of the body used to attend to what someone is saying) stands in for the attention given to the speaker.

The pen is mightier than the sword.
—Edward Bulwer-Lytoon

The act of communicating using the written word is represented by the instrument used to write that word. The act of communicating via power and warfare is represented by the weapon used to wage war.

We can even find metonymy in the Bible, which often uses various body parts to refer to the words and deeds of men and of God:

The tongue of the righteous is choice silver;
  the heart of the wicked is of little worth.
—Proverbs 10:20

Here, Solomon uses the tongue to represent the words spoken by the righteous (Notice the metaphor!). The heart refers to the desires and will of the wicked.

Like the other figures of speech we have studied, a fresh metonymy can substitute a vivid and concrete picture for the subject idea. Choose an important and easily recognizable attribute to use as a metonymy.

You may have noticed that metonymy, like metaphor, uses one word in place of another. These two rhetorical devices do have an important difference. A metaphor can stand in for its subject because of some similarity between them. A metonymy does not rely on similarity, but rather on being near to or associated with its subject.

Lesson 5: Metonymy

I. Appreciating Metonymy

A. Explain the following examples of metonymy.

1. The suits on Wall Street have brought the economy to the brink of disaster.

   a. Underline the metonymy. What does it refer to?

   b. How are the metonomy and its reference related?

2. The Redcoats are coming!

   a. Underline the metonymy. What does it refer to?

   b. How are the metonomy and its reference related?

3. "Houston, we have a problem."
   — From the crew of the ill-fated Apollo 13 mission

   a. Underline the metonymy. What does it refer to?

   b. How are the metonomy and its reference related?

4. By the sweat of your face you shall eat bread ...
   — Genesis 3:19

   a. Underline the metonymy. What does it refer to?

   b. How are the metonomy and its reference related?

5. That in black ink my love may still shine bright.
   — William Shakespeare, "Sonnet 65"

   a. Underline the metonymy. What does it refer to?

   b. How are the metonomy and its reference related?

II. Writing Metonymies

A. Replace the words in brackets with a word closely related to or suggested by the original words and explain the metonymy.

1. I love listening to [medium for storing music].

    a. What does the metonymy refer to?

2. The [book-lending institution] called to say you have an overdue book.

    a. What does the metonymy refer to?

3. The [place where the crops grow] is ripe for the harvest.

    a. What does the metonymy refer to?

4. You can't fight [the headquarters of local government].

    a. What does the metonymy refer to?

5. My [body part used for smelling] led me straight to the freshly baked cookies.

    a. What does the metonymy refer to?

6. The artist has a good [body part used for seeing] for landscapes.

    a. What does the metonymy refer to?

LESSON 6

If you want to spot Oliver at the orchestra concert tomorrow night, just look for the strings.

You'd have a hard time finding Oliver if you were looking for string. But the strings on the violins might lead you right to him. One part of one instrument is substituted for the whole section of stringed instruments. This part-for-whole synecdoche is the most common type, but you can also make a whole-to-part substitution like this:

The rally attracted so many people that the organizers had to call the law to help keep order.

In this whole-for-part synecdoche, the word "law" stands in for individual police officers.

Sometimes a synecdoche substitutes the material that an item is made from for the item itself, as in this example:

The United States won gold at the Olympics.

The word "gold" stands in for the medal made of gold. Did you also catch the whole-to-part synecdoche that refers to the gold-medal athletes by the name of their country?

Another common type of synecdoche substitutes a specific brand for the general category of product, as in these examples:

Kleenex for facial tissues: Please pass me a Kleenex.

synecdoche

si-NEK-duh-kee

From Greek
syn- "with"
ek "out"
dekhesthai "to receive"

A representation of the whole by naming one of its parts, or vice versa.

Xerox® for photocopy: Will you Xerox this for me?

Hoover® for vacuum cleaner: Today I'm going to Hoover the carpets. (This is more common in England.)

ChapStick® for lip balm: The weather is so dry that I apply ChapStick® several times each day.

Synecdoche is very similar to metonymy and is sometimes considered a subcategory of metonymy. Unlike metonymy, which substitutes something *associated* with the subject, a synecdoche substitutes something that is a *part* of the subject. In reality, the line between the two is somewhat fuzzy and depends on one's interpretation. If you're having trouble telling them apart, ask yourself if the two terms are part of the same whole. If so, it's a synecdoche. If not, you have a metonymy. Try it out:

"All hands on deck!" the captain called.

"Give a hand for this fine performer!" the Master of Ceremonies called.

In the first example, the word "hands" is standing in for "sailors." Since hands are part of the sailors, this is a synecdoche. In the second example, the word "hands" is standing in for "applause"—something you do with your hands. Since applause and hands are not part of the same thing, this is a metonymy.

Like metonymy, a synecdoche must be constructed with care. Don't use just any part of the whole to substitute for the whole. Use an important part that is most nearly connected to the subject in view. It just wouldn't be the same if the captain summoned his crew with, "All big toes on deck!"

Why might an author or speaker use a synecdoche? In a good synecdoche, the substituted idea is often more interesting or clear than the subject idea. In this way, synecdoches, like the other devices of association, make our writing and speaking come alive and communicate clearly to others.

I. Appreciating Synecdoche

A. Explain the following examples of synecdoche.

1. I've finally saved enough money for a new set of wheels.

   a. Underline the synecdoche. What does it refer to?

   b. How are the synecdoche and its reference related?

2. It is surprising how many great men and women a small house will contain. I have had twenty-five or thirty souls, with their bodies at once under my roof ...
   —Henry David Thoreau, *Walden*

   a. Underline the synecdoche. What does it refer to?

   b. How are the synecdoche and its reference related?

3. You have said, "Seek my face." My heart says to you, "Your face, LORD, do I seek."
   —Psalm 27:8

   a. Underline the synecdoche. What does it refer to?

   b. How are the synecdoche and its reference related?

4. Thy glass will show thee how thy beauties wear,
   Thy dial how thy precious minutes waste;
   —William Shakespeare, "Sonnet 77"

   a. Underline the synecdoche. What does it refer to?

   b. How are the synecdoche and its reference related?

B. Metonymy or Synecdoche? Explain your choice.

1. Dad works hard to bring home the bacon.

2. "We won't know what the conditions are like until we have boots on the ground," the general reported.

3. He spent the entire evening reading Shakespeare.

4. The rancher lost one-hundred head of cattle in the tornado.

5. He lent a sympathetic ear to his downcast friend.

6. Faint heart never won fair lady.

7. "Take thy face hence."
   —Macbeth in William Shakespeare, *Macbeth*, Act 5, Scene 3

8. "I'll lug the guts into the neighbour room."
   —Hamlet in William Shakespeare, *Hamlet*, Act 3, Scene 4

Lesson 6: Synecdoche | 33

II. Writing Synecdoches

A. **Replace the words in brackets with a part or whole associated with the original words and explain the synecdoche.**

1. Give us this day our daily [basic food to sustain life].
   —Matthew 6:11

   a. What does the synecdoche refer to?

2. Let's go out and grab a [small portion of food] to eat.

   a. What does the synecdoche refer to?

3. I need a [covering of a house] over my head.

   a. What does the synecdoche refer to?

4. We've invited the president of the club to come and say a [single unit of speech].

   a. What does the synecdoche refer to?

5. Tomorrow is graduation, and you're invited to see me [cross the stage and receive my diploma].

   a. What does the synecdoche refer to?

6. He drew his [hard metal] and faced his opponent bravely.

   a. What does the synecdoche refer to?

LESSON 7

I. Identifying Rhetorical Devices

A. Match the rhetorical devices to their definitions:

1. Attributing human qualities to something that is not human:

   _____

2. A reference to an object or concept by using a word closely related to or suggested by the original word:

   _____

3. An implied comparison made by referring to one thing as another:

   _____

4. A representation of the whole by naming one of its parts, or vice versa:

   _____

5. A short, informal reference to a famous person or event:

   _____

6. An explicit comparison of two unlike things, often employing "like" or "as":

   _____

Review

Allusion
Metaphor
Metonymy
Personification
Simile
Synecdoche

II. Recognizing Rhetorical Devices

A. Identify the rhetorical devices used in the following examples.

1. Wisdom cries aloud in the street,
   in the markets she raises her voice.
   —Proverbs 1:20

2. "The burger and fries left without paying," complained the waitress.

3. When forty winters shall besiege thy brow,
   And dig deep trenches in thy beauty's field . . .
   —William Shakespeare, "Sonnet 2"

4. "Shall I keep your hogs, and eat husks with them? What prodigal portion have I spent, that I should come to such penury?"
   —Orlando in William Shakespeare, *As You Like It*, Act 1, Scene 1

5. Like the lake, my serenity is rippled but not ruffled.
   —Henry David Thoreau, *Walden*

6. From Stettin in the Baltic to Trieste in the Adriatic, an iron curtain has descended across the continent.
   —Winston Churchill, 1946

B. Underline and identify the rhetorical devices used in the following passages.

1. Psalm 23

The LORD is my shepherd; I shall not want.

He makes me lie down in green pastures.

   He leads me beside still waters.

He restores my soul.

   He leads me in paths of righteousness for his name's sake.

Even though I walk through the valley of the shadow of death,

   I will fear no evil, for you are with me;

   your rod and your staff, they comfort me.

You prepare a table before me in the presence of my enemies;

   you anoint my head with oil; my cup overflows.

Surely goodness and mercy shall follow me all the days of my life,

   and I shall dwell in the house of the LORD forever.

2. A Book
Emily Dickinson

He ate and drank the precious words,
His spirit grew robust;
He knew no more that he was poor,
Nor that his frame was dust.

He danced along the dingy days,
And this bequest of wings
Was but a book. What liberty
A loosened spirit brings!

The author says a book is

_____, and

_____.

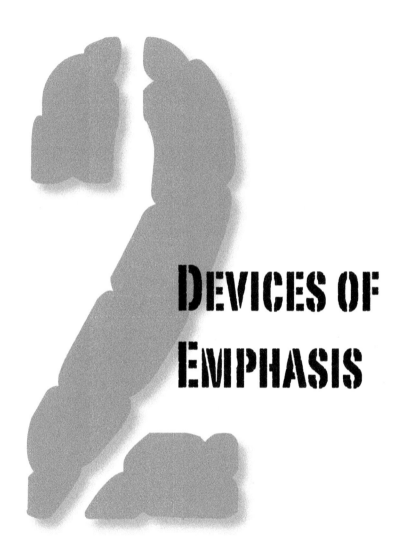

Devices of Emphasis

LESSON 8

climax

KLI-maks

From Greek
klîmax "ladder"

Arranging ideas expressed in words, phrases or clauses in order of increasing importance.

> Our new puppy, Beau, went crazy in my room yesterday. He chewed up three of my pens, a notebook, my favorite pair of sneakers, and my iPod!

You can see that Beau's misdeeds are arranged in order of value and importance. A puppy chewing up a pen is not a big deal. A puppy chewing up an iPod is a really big deal. Listing all of Beau's escapades in order of severity turns up the volume on Oliver's annoyance as he tells his friends what happened to his things.

Climax is a powerful device. Each item in a list builds on the previous one with rising intensity. As your reader reaches the last thought, you have prepared him to recognize its full importance. Arranging items in random order, on the other hand, puts them all on the same plane of importance.

Read about the Beau's escapades again, with the catalog of his destruction in random order:

> Our new puppy, Beau, went crazy in my room yesterday. He chewed up a notebook, my iPod, my favorite pair of sneakers, and three of my pens!

This random list lacks the impact of the example using climax. This might be safer for Beau, but not as satisfying for the reader!

Imagine the effect of this famous example of climax if it were reordered from:

I came, I saw, I conquered.

—Julius Caesar

to:

I came, I conquered, I saw.

It just doesn't have the same ring, does it?

Climax is common in the Bible, as you can see in the following examples:

I am the way, and the truth, and the life.

—John 14:6

So now faith, hope, and love abide, these three; but the greatest of these is love.

—1 Corinthians 13:13

Climax is an especially effective tool in public speaking. The increasing importance of each successive word or phrase causes the audience to anticipate the importance of the speaker's final point. Speakers often use climax in conjunction with asyndeton (the absence of conjunctions) and polysyndeton (multiple conjunctions), which we will study in the next two lessons.

Lesson 8: Climax | 43

I. Appreciating Climax

A. Explain the following examples of climax.

1. "General Secretary Gorbachev, if you seek peace, if you seek prosperity for the Soviet Union and Eastern Europe, if you seek liberalization: Come here to this gate! Mr. Gorbachev, open this gate! Mr. Gorbachev, tear down this wall!"
   —Ronald Reagan, speech to the people of West Berlin, 1987

   a. Underline the three ideas of the climax.

   b. Explain how they build in importance.

2. "In expressing aspirations, in seeking practical plans, in translating humanity's new concept of righteousness and justice and its hatred of war into recommended action we are ready most heartily to unite, but every commitment must be made in the exercise of our national sovereignty."
   —Warren G. Harding, Inaugural Address, 1921

   a. Underline the three ideas of the climax.

   b. Explain how they build in importance.

3. In the beginning was the Word, and the Word was with God, and the Word was God.
   —John 1:1-2 (King James Version)

   a. Underline the three ideas of the climax.

   b. Explain how they build in importance.

II. Writing Climaxes

A. The Missing iPod
1. Make a list of at least four places where Charlotte looked for her missing iPod:

2. Now, write a sentence using climax.

3. What was the reasoning behind the ordering of the places? How did you use climax for emphasis?

B. The Lingering Hiccups

1. Make a list of at least four things Oliver tried in order to get rid of his hiccups:

2. Now, write a sentence using climax.

3. What was the reasoning behind the ordering of the places? How did you use climax for emphasis?

LESSON 9

asyndeton

a-SIN-duh-ton

From Greek
a "not"
syn "together"
dein "to bind"

Omitting conjunctions between words, phrases, or clauses.

Mr. Penn was a real Renaissance man, excelling in music, art, literature, astronomy, architecture.

The list of Mr. Penn's accomplishments is quite impressive. But notice something else. It sounds like this list could go on; it sounds like it's not complete. That's because of the deliberate omission of any conjunctions — called asyndeton. When you use this device, it sounds as if you are reeling off a list that could always go on a few more items.

How does adding a conjunction to the end of the list change the feel of the sentence?

Mr. Penn was a real Renaissance man, excelling in music, art, literature, astronomy, and architecture.

Mr. Penn seems a little less accomplished in this example, as if this list is the sum total of his interests.

Sometimes leaving out the conjunction between short phrases gives the impression that the writer or speaker is searching for just the right word — like he is "trying out" words to see if they accurately convey what he is trying to say:

Winning the championship was the happiest day of my life; I was amazed, elated, overwhelmed.

This asyndetic list (a list without conjunctions) lets us see the writer's thought process as he struggles to find the best word to describe his emotions.

When used with climax, asyndeton is especially effective:

"You must read these books, know these books, love these books, in order to do well in this class," Oliver's English teacher said on the first day of school.

Here the asyndeton makes the climax stronger and more forceful.

Asyndeton is particularly effective when spoken and is commonly used in speeches. Do you recognize either of these famous speeches?

"...and that government of the people, by the people, for the people shall not perish from the earth."
—Abraham Lincoln, Gettysburg Address

"Let every nation know, whether it wishes us well or ill, that we shall pay any price, bear any burden, meet any hardship, support any friend, oppose any foe to assure the survival and the success of liberty."
—John F. Kennedy, Inaugural Address 1961

Asyndeton quickens the rhythm of a spoken passage, making it more memorable. Try reading those stirring lines out loud with conjunctions between each phrase and you'll see the difference.

Use asyndeton in your writing to give the feeling of an incomplete listing, searching for the best word, or to make the use of climax even more powerful.

Lesson 9: Asyndeton

I. Appreciating Asyndeton

A. Explain the following examples of asyndeton. What effect is produced by the asyndeton?

1. "Anyway, like I was saying, shrimp is the fruit of the sea. You can barbecue it, boil it, broil it, bake it, sauté it. Dey's uh, shrimp-kabobs, shrimp creole, shrimp gumbo. Pan fried, deep fried, stir-fried. There's pineapple shrimp, lemon shrimp, coconut shrimp, pepper shrimp, shrimp soup, shrimp stew, shrimp salad, shrimp and potatoes, shrimp burger, shrimp sandwich. That—that's about it."
   —Bubba in *Forrest Gump*

2. "We shall go on to the end, we shall fight in France, we shall fight on the seas and oceans, we shall fight with growing confidence and growing strength in the air, we shall defend our Island, whatever the cost may be, we shall fight on the beaches, we shall fight on the landing grounds, we shall fight in the fields and in the streets, we shall fight in the hills; we shall never surrender. . ."
   —Winston Churchill, Speech delivered to House of Commons, 1940

3. "Duty, Honor, Country: Those three hallowed words reverently dictate what you ought to be, what you can be, what you will be. They are your rallying points: to build courage when courage seems to fail; to regain faith when there seems to be little cause for faith; to create hope when hope becomes forlorn."
   —General Douglas MacArthur, speech delivered at West Point, 1962

II. Writing Asyndeton

A. **Convert the following sentences to asyndeton. Explain how the "flavor" of the sentence has changed.**

1. My mind was a whirl as I contemplated all the supplies I would need for my science project—flower pots, soil, seeds, ruler, poster board, and markers.

2. Going out for the varsity team stretched me to the limit with strength training, and aerobic training, and endless practices, and painful injuries, and sitting on the bench, and last-minute substitutions, and adrenaline moments.

B. **Write a sentence using asyndeton to describe each of the following:**

1. The things that went wrong on a bad day.

2. The things that fill up your very heavy backpack.

LESSON 10

> After years of dreaming and thinking and planning and saving and working, Mrs. Penn's dream of becoming a vet became a reality.

Mrs. Penn sure has worked hard! What part of this sentence helps us understand how difficult it has been for her to become a vet? One small word, which we often overlook: *and*. We feel how far she has come because we hear "and...and...and"—a pile of *and*'s, in fact. They pull those big verbs after them—dreaming, planning, saving. By the end of the sentence, seeing this big pile, we understand just how hard Mrs. Penn has worked to achieve her goal.

Polysyndeton, the opposite of asyndeton, is the use of conjunctions between each word, phrase, or clause in a sentence. While a list using asyndeton sounds open-ended and spontaneous, a list using polysyndeton sounds comprehensive and deliberate.

Even the rhythm of the sentences is changed from the quick, staccato rhythm of asyndeton to the slow and steady drum beat of polysyndeton. In fact, that's how polysyndeton works. The repeated use of the conjunction slows the reader down so he can absorb all the content of the sentence.

When we use multiple conjunctions to join words, phrases, or clauses, the conjunctions show that the linked items are equal in some way. Using *and* to pile up meaning is the most common polysyndeton, as in this famous speech by the fictitious George Bailey:

polysyndeton

pol-ee-SIN-duh-ton

From Greek
poly "many"
syn "together"
dein "to bind"

Using conjunctions between each word, phrase, or clause.

"Just remember this, Mr. Potter: that this rabble you're talking about, they do most of the working and paying and living and dying in this community. Well, is it too much to have them work and pay and live and die in a couple of decent rooms and a bath?"
—George Bailey in *It's a Wonderful Life*

Other conjunctions serve different purposes. The repeated use of *or* emphasizes different alternatives:

Because they know what they're doing won't work, or is wrongheaded, or confused, or cowardly, or cynical, or just another way to dither, or will more likely yield bad outcomes than good.
—Peggy Noonan in *The Wall Street Journal*, Feb 22, 2002

The repeated use of *nor* is a negative way to list alternatives.

Neither snow, nor rain, nor heat, nor gloom of night stays these couriers from the swift completion of their appointed rounds.
—Inscription, New York City Post Office, adapted from Herodotus

Use polysyndeton in your writing to slow down the rhythm of your sentence or to emphasize or intensify the impact of a list of items.

I. Appreciating Polysyndeton

A. Explain the following examples of polysyndeton. What effect is produced by the polysyndeton?

1. No free man shall be taken or imprisoned or dispossessed, or outlawed or exiled, or in any way destroyed, nor will we go upon him, nor will we send against him except by the lawful judgment of his peers or by the law of the land.
   —*Magna Carta* Clause 39, 1215

2. Behold, the LORD maketh the earth empty, and maketh it waste, and turneth it upside down, and scattereth abroad the inhabitants thereof.
   —Isaiah 24:1 (King James Version)

3. In an hour unlooked for by Men this doom befell, on the nine and thirtieth day since the passing of the fleets. Then suddenly fire burst from the Meneltarma, and there came a mighty wind and a tumult of the earth, and the sky reeled, and the hills slid, and Númenor went down into the sea, with all its children and its wives and its maidens and its ladies proud; and all its gardens and its halls and its towers, its tombs and its riches, and its jewels and its webs and its things painted and carven, and its laughter and its mirth and its music, its wisdom and its lore; they vanished forever.
   —J.R.R. Tolkien, *The Silmarillion*

II. Writing Climax, Asyndeton, Polysyndeton

A. Construct a sentence using either an asyndetic or polysyndetic list of the following items. Use climax to enhance the effect of your sentence.

1. A whirlwind road trip: 11 states, 16 hotel rooms, 53 greasy cafes, 2 sets of tires, 68 cups of black coffee, 3491 miles

   What is the effect of the devices you chose?

2. A leisurely vacation cruise: ports-of-call, colorful markets, endless buffets, sparkling conversation, pool side lounging

   What is the effect of the devices you chose?

LESSON 11

irony

i-ruh-nee

From Greek *eironeia* "feigned ignorance"

An incongruity between what might be expected and what actually occurs or is said.

"Well, I don't think my essay is very good," Oliver told his teacher," but at least it's 200 words shorter than the required word count."

Oliver's bragging about the shortness of his essay is ironic. We would expect Oliver to be ashamed that his paper was too short, but instead he sounds proud of it. For some mysterious reason, this is just funny. It satisfies our sense of proportion in a way we can't explain.

Saying one thing and meaning the opposite is the simplest form of rhetorical (or verbal) irony. A specific type of irony called ironic simile also communicates the opposite of what it means, as in this example:

The teacher's explanation of long division was as clear as mud.

It looks like the simile is going to tell us how clear the lesson was, but it ends up telling us that it was not clear at all.

Ironic statements that say the opposite of what they mean surprise us, make us stop and think, and actually underline the truth.

Besides rhetorical or verbal irony described above, irony comes in other flavors:

Dramatic Irony—irony in speeches or situations in a play that is understood by the audience but not the characters in the play. The most famous example of dramatic irony is the play *Oedipus Rex* by the Greek playwright Sophocles. The play opens with Oedipus, the ruler of Thebes, declaring that he will find the man whose sins have brought a plague on the city. The audience knows what Oedipus does not: he himself is that man.

Situational Irony—a discrepancy between the expected results of a situation and the actual results. The author O. Henry gave us the classic example of situational irony in his short story *The Gift of the Magi*. A young man and his wife, deeply in love, are too poor to buy Christmas presents for each other. The wife sells her beautiful long hair for money to buy a watch-fob for her husband's heirloom pocket watch. Meanwhile, the husband has sold his watch to buy her a set of combs for her hair.

Socratic Irony—pretending to be ignorant and eager to learn in a discussion. This form of irony is named for its most famous practitioner, the Greek philosopher Socrates, who was actually teaching his fellow Athenians when he claimed to be learning from them.

All forms of irony share one thing: a gap between what is said and what is true. The gap itself highlights what is meant. Writing irony is a notoriously tricky endeavor. The gap between the actual words and the meaning must be significant, not just a factual error or a lie. More importantly, the effective use of irony depends on the audience's ability to recognize the gap. If your reader doesn't recognize the irony you can end up being misunderstood.

I. Appreciating Irony

A. Explain the following examples of irony.

1. Truth is stranger than fiction, but it is because Fiction is obliged to stick to possibilities; Truth isn't.
   —Mark Twain

   a. Would you expect truth or fiction to be stranger?

   b. Which does Mark Twain think is stranger?

2. Water, water, everywhere,
   And all the boards did shrink;
   Water, water, every where,
   Nor any drop to drink
   —Samuel Coleridge, *The Rime of the Ancient Mariner*

   a. What would you expect to result from being surrounded by water?

   b. What actually occurred?

   c. What type of irony is this?

3. And over his head they put the charge against him, which read, "This is Jesus, the King of the Jews."
   —Matthew 27:37

   a. What did Pilate mean by the accusation?

   b. What was the hidden truth?

   c. What type of irony is this?

II. Writing Irony

A. Complete these examples of ironic simile.

1. That joke was as funny as . . .

2. That dog is as friendly as . . .

3. Your room is as clean as . . .

B. Complete these examples of situational irony.

1. I was going to a speech about punctuality, but . . .

2. I was almost finished writing my article about eating healthy food, but . . .

3. It took me eight hours to get here by plane, train, and automobile, but now I'm ready to speak to you about . . .

LESSON 12

Oliver looked at the mess left by our new puppy's chewing spree. "Well, it looks like Beau had a busy day," he said, as Mom held up her favorite (now tattered) sweater.

When faced with the results of Beau's "busy day," Oliver doesn't need to point out the grave damage or even attempt to exaggerate the damage. Imagine the effect if Oliver had surveyed the room and said:

I see that Beau has damaged four items.

Or:

It looks like Beau has chewed up everything in the house!

Instead, he described Beau's rampage as a "busy day," providing ironic emphasis. Oddly enough, understating the extent of the damage draws attention to it by tricking us into imagining the scene ourselves. Often we imagine it to be even worse than it is. The more extreme the subject, the more effective the understatement.

Besides adding ironic emphasis, understatement helps you to be modest. It's never good to toot your own horn, so if you must comment on your abilities or accomplishments, understatement is the way to go. Compare:

Yes, I was the star of the yesterday's game.

Yes, I made a small contribution to yesterday's victory.

understatement

UN-der-state-ment

Expressing an idea as less important than it actually is.

Similarly, understatement is helpful in persuasive writing or speaking. When we use understatement to present our claims we create trust between ourselves and our audience. They do not feel that we are exaggerating to make a point. Which of the following examples is more convincing?

Studying rhetorical devices is the most important thing you will ever do.

Or:

Studying rhetorical devices may help you become a better writer.

Understating your claims shows attention to detail as well as respect for your reader by allowing him or her to decide the strong points of your argument.

Although understatement often provides humor or ironic emphasis, it is also simply a means of effective writing. Understatement forces you to observe and describe your subject with details and specifics rather than the hype of meaningless modifiers and exclamation points. Lazy writers use adverbs to convince their readers that a subject is noteworthy rather than using details to show why we should pay attention. The key to understated writing is to provide the details your reader needs in order to draw his or her own conclusions.

Lesson 12: Understatement | 59

I. Appreciating Understatement

A. Explain the following examples of understatement.

1. The reports of my death are greatly exaggerated.
   —Mark Twain

   a. What is the reality?

   b. How is it understated?

2. "No, 'tis not so deep as a well, nor so wide as a church-door; but 'tis enough,'twill serve: ask for me to-morrow, and you shall find me a grave man."
   —Mercutio describes his mortal wound in William Shakespeare, *Romeo and Juliet*, Act 2, Scene 1

   a. What is the reality?

   b. How is it understated?

3. "I am just going outside and may be some time."
   —Captain Lawrence Oates, before walking out into a blizzard to face certain death when his ill health threatened the survival of his companions on their Antarctic expedition in 1912.

   a. What is the reality?

   b. How is it understated?

4. "This structure has novel features which are of considerable biological interest."
   —J. Watson and F. Crick reporting their discovery of the double helix structure of DNA, for which they won the Nobel Prize in 1962.

   a. What is the reality?

   b. How is it understated?

II. Writing Understatement

A. Change the following statements to understatements.

1. My dog is fat.
    My dog is on the big side.

2. She set a new team record.

3. The food is inedible.

4. He's the smartest kid in class.

B. Write a sentence using understatement to describe each of the following situations.

1. Your reaction to a friend's <u>good idea</u> for a Friday night activity.

2. Your reaction to a friend's <u>bad idea</u> for a Friday night activity.

LESSON 13

litotes

LI-tuh-teez

From Greek
litos "plain, small, meager"

Expressing a thought by denying its opposite.

Oliver held up his ruined iPod, not unhappily. "I guess this means I can get the newest model now."

It's true that Oliver seems happy to learn that his iPod has been ruined, but by denying the opposite of that sentiment we show that he has mixed feelings about his loss. He likes the idea of a new iPod but knows that his old one will be expensive to replace. Read this sentence again, this time without litotes, and see if it does justice to Oliver's attitude:

Oliver held up his ruined iPod, happily. "I guess this means I can get the newest model now."

Litotes is a form of understatement and like understatement it emphasizes meaning by highlighting the gap between what is meant and what is stated.

In litotic speech, the speaker's words convey less emotion than is actually felt. This device is common in Old English poetry like *Beowulf* and Icelandic sagas—cultures known for their stoical restraint.

> "That [sword] was not useless to the warrior now."
> —*Beowulf*

The use of litotes is not uncommon (a common litotes!) in everyday expressions like:

Not bad.
This is no small problem.
It's no fun to be sick.
Not a bad day's work.

Like understatement, litotes can also serve to downplay one's accomplishments in a modest way, as in this example:

I'm no rocket scientist, but I think I can help you with your calculus homework.

Litotes can also soften the blow of an uncomfortable truth as in this example:

She's not the friendliest person I've ever met.

You're probably familiar with these combinations of metaphor and litotes that are also used to "soften the blow."

He's not the brightest bulb in the pack.
She's not the sharpest knife in the drawer.

But probably the most famous litotes in history is attributed to Queen Victoria, responding to an off-color joke by one of her grooms-in-waiting:

We are not amused.

By the way, the plural of litotes is — litotes!

Lesson 13: Litotes

I. Appreciating Litotes

A. Explain the following examples of litotes.

1. For consider your calling, brothers: not many of you were wise according to worldly standards, not many were powerful, not many were of noble birth.
   —1 Corinthians 1:26
   a. Underline the litotes.
   b. What does it mean?

2. "Let him fly far, Not in this land shall he remain uncaught."
   —Gloucester in William Shakespeare, *King Lear*, Act 2, Scene 1
   a. Underline the litotes.
   b. What does it mean?

3. "I am a Jew, from Tarsus in Cilicia, a citizen of no obscure city."
   —Acts 21:39
   a. Underline the litotes.
   b. What does it mean?

4. To say that he was not startled, or that his blood was not conscious of a terrible sensation to which it had been a stranger from infancy, would be untrue.
   —Charles Dickens, *A Christmas Carol*
   a. Underline the litotes.
   b. What does it mean?

II. Writing Litotes

A. Change the underlined phrase to a negative expression of its opposite.

1. I was <u>very upset.</u>

    I was not happy.

2. I'm afraid that <u>only a few</u> of you passed the test.

3. It <u>will be hard</u> to pass the course if you don't study.

4. It <u>is possible</u> for you to still pass with flying colors.

B. Write a sentence using litotes to describe each of the following situations.

1. Your reaction to a friend's <u>good idea</u> for a Friday night activity.

2. Your reaction to a friend's <u>bad idea</u> for a Friday night activity.

LESSON 14

While some dogs may eat you out of house and home, we're more concerned about Beau eating our house and home!

That's quite a picture isn't it? This extravagant exaggeration is not intended to be taken literally, but it does convey the point that Beau likes to eat.

We've now learned three different ways to draw attention to Beau's large appetite:

Beau certainly has a healthy appetite.
(understatement)
Beau's appetite is certainly not puny.
(litotes)
Beau is so hungry he could eat a horse!
(hyperbole)

Each of these examples expresses our meaning more vividly than simply saying that Beau has a large appetite.

The media and advertisers bombard us with hyperbole every day. Sometimes we call this hype, or media hype. (The word "hype" comes from hyperbole.) We hear so many exaggerated descriptions that we ignore hyperbole as a figure of speech, and it loses its power.

Bright Star Shampoo gives your hair a mirror-like shine!

ComBlast provides lightening-fast internet connection!

Used carefully, however, hyperbole is still an effective rhetorical device that draws attention to our meaning in a pointed or witty way. Use hyperbole to spice up your informal

hyperbole

hy-PER-buh-lee

From Greek
hyper "over, beyond"
ballein "to throw"

Extravagant exaggeration not intended to be taken literally.

writing, but remember that hyperbole must be an obvious exaggeration. If the statement is true, then it is not a hyperbole:

The Sears Tower is the tallest building in the United States.

If the statement is only slightly exaggerated, then it could possibly be taken literally by mistake:

If I've told you once, I've told you three times to pick up your shoes!

Make sure that the exaggeration is great enough that it is obviously hyperbole.

Hyperbole works most effectively when used with a calm tone to emphasize a point in a witty way.

While I did ask for a short haircut, I must admit I was hoping to avoid premature baldness.

I'll have plenty of time to finish all this homework. Eating and sleeping are highly overrated.

Although hyperbole works well in creative writing, avoid using it in formal writing or business writing.

I. Appreciating Hyperbole

A. Explain the following examples of hyperbole.

1. "It is easier for a camel to go through the eye of a needle than for a rich person to enter the kingdom of God."
   —Matthew 19:24

   a. Underline the hyperbole.
   b. What truth is the hyperbole intended to highlight?

2. By the rude bridge that arched the flood,
   Their flag to April's breeze unfurled,
   Here once the embattled farmers stood,
   And fired the shot heard round the world.
   —Ralph Waldo Emerson, "The Concord Hymn"

   a. Underline the hyperbole.
   b. What truth is the hyperbole intended to highlight?

3. "What hands are here? ha! they pluck out mine eyes.
   Will all great Neptune's ocean wash this blood
   Clean from my hand? No, this my hand will rather
   The multitudinous seas incarnadine,
   Making the green one red."
   —Macbeth in William Shakespeare, *Macbeth*, Act 2, Scene 2

   a. Underline the hyperbole.
   b. What truth is the hyperbole intended to highlight?

II. Writing Hyperbole

A. Finish these sentences using hyperbole.

1. I had so many chores to do on Saturday ...

2. After the big game I was so tired ...

3. I am so fast at texting ...

4. I am so tired of homework ...

B. Write a sentence using hyperbole to describe each of the following situations.

1. How happy you were when you made the team.

2. How big your dog is.

LESSON 15

I. Identifying Rhetorical Devices

A. Match the rhetorical devices to their definitions:

1. Expressing an idea as less important than it actually is:
   _____

2. Arranging ideas expressed in words, phrases or clauses in order of increasing importance:
   _____

3. Using conjunctions between each word, phrase, or clause:
   _____

4. Extravagant exaggeration not intended to be taken literally:
   _____

5. An incongruity between what might be expected and what actually occurs or is said:
   _____

6. Omitting conjunctions between words, phrases, or clauses:
   _____

7. Expressing a thought by denying its opposite:
   _____

Review

Asyndeton
Climax
Hyperbole
Irony
Litotes
Polysyndeton
Understatement

II. Recognizing Rhetorical Devices

A. Identify the devices of emphasis used in the following examples.

1. He kept slipping into snow drifts, and skidding on frozen puddles, and tripping over fallen logs, and sliding down steep banks, and barking his shins against rocks.
   —C.S. Lewis, *The Lion, the Witch, and the Wardrobe*

2. Harris and I had been hard at work on our German during several weeks at that time, and although we had made good progress, it had been accomplished under great difficulty and annoyance, for three of our teachers had died in the mean time.
   —Mark Twain, "The Awful German Lanugage"

3. But the fruit of the Spirit is love, joy, peace, patience, kindness, goodness, faithfulness, gentleness, self-control; against such things there is no law.
   —Galatians 5:22-23

4. The one who stood guard was dangerous and watchful, warden of that trove buried under earth: no easy bargain would be made in that place by any man.
   —*Beowulf*

5. When I see someone coming towards me with the obvious intention of doing me good, I run a mile.
   —Henry David Thoreau

6. Renounce my love, my life, myself—and you.
   —Alexander Pope, "Eloisa to Abelard"

B. Identify the rhetorical devices used in the following examples.

1. Killing time is not murder—it's suicide.

2. As smoke is driven away, so you shall drive them away;
   as wax melts before fire, so the wicked shall perish before God!
   —Psalm 68:2

3. Courtship consists in a fellow running after a woman until she has caught him.

4. A cut-purse of the empire and the rule,
   That from a shelf the precious diadem stole,
   And put it in his pocket!
   —Hamlet in William Shakespeare, *Hamlet*, Act 3, Scene 4

5. No, but you . . . you . . . you're thinking of this place all wrong. As if I had the money back in a safe. The money's not here. Your money's in Joe's house . . . right next to yours. And in the Kennedy house, and Mrs. Macklin's house, and a hundred others.
   —George Bailey in *It's a Wonderful Life*

6. Wisdom cries aloud in the street,
   in the markets she raises her voice;
   —Proverbs 1:20

C. Underline and identify the rhetorical devices used by Charles Dickens in this passage from *A Christmas Carol*.

Oh! But he was a tight-fisted hand at the grind-stone, Scrooge! a squeezing, wrenching, grasping, scraping, clutching, covetous, old sinner! Hard and sharp as flint, from which no steel had ever struck out generous fire; secret, and self-contained, and solitary as an oyster. The cold within him froze his old features, nipped his pointed nose, shriveled his cheek, stiffened his gait; made his eyes red, his thin lips blue and spoke out shrewdly in his grating voice. A frosty rime was on his head, and on his eyebrows, and his wiry chin. He carried his own low temperature always about with him; he iced his office in the dogdays; and didn't thaw it one degree at Christmas.

External heat and cold had little influence on Scrooge. No warmth could warm, no wintry weather chill him. No wind that blew was bitterer than he, no falling snow was more intent upon its purpose, no pelting rain less open to entreaty. Foul weather didn't know where to have him. The heaviest rain, and snow, and hail, and sleet, could boast of the advantage over him in only one respect. They often "came down" handsomely, and Scrooge never did.

3 Devices of Balance & Restatement

LESSON 16

parallelism

PAR-uh-lel-iz-uhm

From Greek
parallelos "side-by-side"

Using the same pattern of words to present multiple ideas of equal importance.

> Oliver was a pretty normal kid. He usually did his homework, rarely cleaned his room, and never ate his peas.

What makes this list so pleasant to read? Although these three character traits aren't anything special, parallelism gives them a catchy rhythm. To list each item, we have an adverb, then a verb, and then a direct object with the possessive word "his" attached. Listing the activities using the same pattern of words makes the list more understandable, gives rhythm and balance to the sentence, and implies the equal importance of each idea. It also makes such a list easier to remember later.

Compare this parallel sentence to the unbalanced version, which presents the multiple ideas using varying structures:

> Oliver was a pretty normal kid. He usually did his homework and didn't like cleaning his room. He also thought peas were gross.

This faulty parallelism sounds clunky because it lacks the patterns that help our minds understand what we read and hear. Faulty parallelism makes our writing difficult to understand because it hides the equal importance of the parallel items.

Parallelism is a versatile tool that can be used with various sentence structures. Look at these examples of parallel elements:

1. Words, phrases, or clauses that are joined by conjunctions.

   Clear <u>writing</u> and <u>speaking</u> help us to communicate successfully.
   We must <u>both say</u> what we mean <u>and mean</u> what we say.

2. Words, phrases, or clauses in a series.

   To communicate effectively you must <u>think logically</u>, <u>write carefully</u>, and <u>speak clearly</u>.
   Our words should be <u>clear</u>, <u>concise</u>, and <u>elegant</u>.

3. Words, phrases, or clauses being compared.

   A <u>boring speech</u> is worse than a <u>bad speech</u>.
   <u>To speak</u> concisely is more difficult than <u>to chatter</u> endlessly.

4. Words, phrases, or clauses joined by a being verb.

   <u>To teach</u> children is <u>to touch</u> lives.
   <u>Seeing</u> is <u>believing</u>.

Parallelism is so basic to good writing that it plays a supporting role in other rhetorical devices, including polysyndeton, aysndeton, anaphora, epistrophe, antithesis, and many others.

Use parallelism when you need to express a series of similar meanings. Parallel structures emphasize the equal importance of the ideas and add balance and beauty to your writing as well.

Addendum:
The rhetorical device called **isocolon** (i-so-CO-lon) includes a succession of clauses of not only similar structure, but also equal length (about the same number of words or syllables).

Climate is what we expect, weather is what we get.
— Mark Twain

I. Appreciating Parallelism

A. Underline the parallel words or phrases in the following examples.

1. Tell me and I forget. Teach me and I may remember. Involve me and I will learn.
   — Benjamin Franklin

2. For my yoke is easy, and my burden is light.
   — Matthew 11:30

3. It is better to go to the house of mourning than to go to the house of feasting.
   — Ecclesiastes 7:2

4. For the support of this declaration, with a firm reliance on the protection of Divine Providence, we mutually pledge to each other our Lives, our Fortunes, and our sacred Honor.
   — Declaration of Independence

5. My study, lined with books, reflects my interests, confines my identity as a writer, and reinforces my sense of what kind of person I consider myself to be.
   — Anthony Storr

6. One must try to temper, to cut, to polish one's soul so as to become a human being.
   — Alexander Solzhenitsyn

II. Writing with Parallelism

A. Complete the following sentences using parallelism by supplying a word or phrase that is parallel to the underlined words.

1. I spent the afternoon <u>cleaning</u> my room, _____ the piano, and _____ my homework.

2. When our puppy Beau escaped, we <u>chased him down</u> the street, _____ the yards, and _____ the fence.

B. Complete the following sentences using parallelism by supplying parallel words or phrases.

1. I love _____, _____, and _____.

2. When looking for a job one should _____, _____, and _____.

C. Rewrite the following sentences to correct for parallelism.

1. I like to play the piano and composing music.

2. On Saturday I spent the day playing video games, listened to music and watched TV.

3. He likes to eat donuts more than eating oatmeal.

4. Seeing is to believe.

LESSON 17

This afternoon Charlotte rushed happily to the library, then sadly returned to her chores.

Although similar to parallelism, a chiasmus inverts the parallelism. Rather than matching the verb and adverb *rushed happily* with *returned sadly*, the second pair is inverted: AB-BA instead of AB-AB.

We could diagram Charlotte's day like this:

Charlotte <u>rushed happily</u>
to the library

and <u>sadly returned</u>
to her chores.

If we visually connect the two verbs and the two adverbs, you can see why the Greek word meaning *crossing* is used to describe this diagonal arrangement of words.

Why would you use chiasmus instead of parallelism? Chiasmus allows you to bring two words or ideas together in order to contrast or emphasize them. In our example above, the chiasmus brings together the words *happily* and *sadly*, drawing our attention to the contrast between Charlotte's two moods.

Likewise, chiasmus might allow you to move the most important word to the end of a sentence for emphasis. Compare these two sentences:

What is learned unwillingly is forgotten gladly.

What is learned unwillingly is gladly forgotten.

chiasmus

ki-AZ-mus

From Greek *khiasmos* "crossing, diagonal arrangment"

Repeating grammatical structures in inverted order.

The chiastic structure places the word *forgotten* in the position of emphasis at the end of the sentence.

Whenever you use parallelism in your writing, try out a chiasmus to see which arrangement is more effective and pleasing.

Addendum:

Note that chiasmus inverts grammatical structures. Sometimes, however, we want to invert repeated words. This is called antimetabole (an-tee-meh-TA-bol-lee). Take a look at these examples:

I meant what I said and I said what I meant.
—Dr. Seuss, Horton Hears a Who

Ask not what your country can do for you, but what you can do for your country.
—John F. Kennedy

East and West do not mistrust each other because we are armed; we're armed because we mistrust each other.
—Ronald Reagan

The term chiasmus is more common than antimetabole and is usually used to designate both devices in modern speech.

Lesson 17: Chiasmus

I. Appreciating Chiasmus

A. Underline the chiastic structures.

1. Whoever sheds the blood of man, by man shall his blood be shed, for God made man in his own image.
   —Genesis 9:6

2. By day the frolic, and the dance by night.
   —Samuel Johnson, "The Vanity of Human Wishes"

3. It is not even the beginning of the end, but is perhaps, the end of the beginning.
   —Winston Churchill

4. Charm is a woman's strength … strength is a man's charm.
   —Havelock Ellis

5. Fair is foul, and foul is fair.
   —Witch in William Shakespeare, *Macbeth*, Act 1, Scene 1

6. Those gallant men will remain often in my thoughts and in my prayers always.
   —General Douglas MacArthur

7. Each throat was parched, and glazed each eye.
   —Samuel Taylor Coleridge, "The Rime of the Ancient Mariner"

8. One should eat to live, not live to eat.
   —Molière, *L'Avare*

II. Writing Chiasmus

A. Change the parallel structures in the following sentences to a chiasmus. Compare the two sentences. Which do you think is more effective?

1. Time may fly when you're having fun, but it races when you're late for school.

2. Go to bed on time and get up when your alarm sounds.

B. Change the chaiastic structures in the following sentences to parallelism. Compare the two sentences. Which do you think is more effective?

1. When beginning a new job, remember to arrive promptly and diligently work.

2. Our puppy Beau chases his tail constantly but rarely catches it.

C. Try your hand at antimetabole by repeating the same words in a different order.

1. It is better to _____ and not _____

   than to _____ and not _____ .

LESSON 18

Charolotte's idea of summer vacation is rest and relaxation; her mother's idea is extra time for chores.

Have you ever noticed that in trying to describe something, we often resort to saying what it's *not* like? That's the power of antithesis. One of the best ways to clarify an idea is to show how it differs from another idea. When we think about contrasting ideas together, we understand both ideas more clearly because of the difference between them.

Antithesis joins two opposing ideas in order to create clarity and emphasis. Presenting the antithesis using parallelism conveys even complex ideas with balance and beauty. Imagine the great wealth of human experience that is captured in these examples of antithesis:

The deeper the sorrow, the greater the joy.

Success makes us proud; failure makes us wise.

The Apostle Paul uses antithesis to describe the threats he faces, giving us a richer understanding of his situation than if he had simply listed the threats:

We are afflicted in every way, but not crushed; perplexed, but not driven to despair; persecuted, but not forsaken; struck down, but not destroyed; always carrying in the body the death of Jesus, so that the life of Jesus may also be manifested in our bodies.
— 2 Corinthians 4:8-10

antithesis

an-TITH-uh-sis

From Greek
anti "against"
tithenai "to place"

Joining together two opposing ideas.

Notice the second antithesis at the end of the verse contrasting the death and the life of Jesus.

Antithesis is also valuable for clarifying the differences between two things, as in these examples:

Love is an ideal thing, marriage a real thing.
—Goethe

An inconvenience is only an adventure wrongly considered; an adventure is an inconvenience rightly considered.
—G. K. Chesterton

Contrasting opposing ideas makes us stop and think about *how* they differ. Notice the parallelism in the first example and the chiasmus in the second example.

Use parallelism, chiasmus, and antithesis to set up contrasts that make ideas rich and memorable in description, persuasion, and motivation.

Lesson 18: Antithesis | 85

I. Appreciating Antithesis

A. Underline the antithetical structures in the following examples. What idea is conveyed by the contrast?

1. That's one small step for a man, one giant leap for mankind.
   — Neil Armstrong, first words spoken on the moon, July 20, 1969

2. To err is human; to forgive, divine.
   — Alexander Pope, "Essay on Criticism"

3. It has been my experience that folks who have no vices have very few virtues.
   — Abraham Lincoln

4. The inherent vice of capitalism is the unequal sharing of blessings; the inherent virtue of socialism is the equal sharing of miseries.
   — Winston Churchill

5. "You have heard that it was said, 'You shall love your neighbor and hate your enemy.' But I say to you, love your enemies and pray for those who persecute you . . ."
   — Matthew 5:43-44

6. "Not that I loved Caesar less, but that I loved Rome more. Had you rather Caesar were living and die all slaves, than that Caesar were dead, to live all free men?"
   — Brutus in William Shakespeare, *Julius Cæsar*, Act 3, Scene 2

II. Writing Antithesis

A. Choose a pair of opposite words and write a sentence showing antithesis.

Nouns:
    joy / sorrow   winter / summer   friend / enemy
    love / hate   silence / noise   morning / evening

1. I love school, but I hate homework!

2.

Adjectives:
    difficult / easy   serious / silly   new / used
    less / more   trilling / boring   safe / dangerous

1.

2.

Verbs (you can change the form of the verb, e.g. walking, walked, to walk):
    walk / run   love / hate   talk / sing
    smile / frown   give / take   live / die

1.

2.

LESSON 19

Mom finally agreed to take us to the beach this summer if we cleaned up our rooms, if we mowed the lawn, and if we finished our summer-school reading.

Mom's list sounds pretty foreboding, partly because of the repeated word at the beginning of each clause. The repeated use of the word *if* stresses the conditional nature of the trip to the beach.

When you repeat a word or words at the beginning of successive clauses, sentences, or lines, you're using a device called anaphora. If you want to emphasize the subject, you can repeat a noun. If you want to emphasize an action, try repeating a verb.

Anaphora fits all of our phrases into the same mold, so that we can build them together to create a coherent picture, as in this famous example of anaphora:

> It was the best of times, it was the worst of times, it was the age of wisdom, it was the age of foolishness, it was the epoch of belief, it was the epoch of incredulity, it was the season of Light, it was the season of Darkness, it was the spring of hope, it was the winter of despair. . .
> —Charles Dickens, *A Tale of Two Cities*

You can see, especially in the following example, that anaphora is a type of parallel structure:

> If we had no winter, the spring would not be so pleasant; if we did not sometimes taste of adversity, prosperity would not be so welcome.
> —Anne Bradstreet

anaphora

uh-NAF-er-uh

From Greek
ana "back"
pherein "to bring or carry"

Repeating a word or words at the beginning of successive clauses, sentences, or lines.

The hypnotic power of repetition can lend an insistent driving rhythm to a speech. We actually anticipate the next line as the momentum of the repetition carries us along.

> We shall go on to the end,
> we shall fight in France,
> we shall fight on the seas and oceans,
> we shall fight with growing confidence and growing strength in the air, we shall defend our Island, whatever the cost may be,
> we shall fight on the beaches,
> we shall fight on the landing grounds,
> we shall fight in the fields and in the streets,
> we shall fight in the hills
> we shall never surrender..."
>
> —Winston Churchill

Anaphora works well for making lists of thoughts, experiences, or ideas. It is like a battering ram: the repeated word or phrase unifies the various ideas it carries into a single driving persuasive force. Repetition naturally grabs and focuses our attention and sears the repeated words or phrases on our minds, making our writing and speaking memorable.

I. Appreciating Anaphora

A. Underline the repeated words or phrases in the following examples. What is the effect of the anaphora?

1. Blessed are the poor in spirit, for theirs is the kingdom of heaven.
   Blessed are those who mourn, for they shall be comforted.
   Blessed are the meek, for they shall inherit the earth.
   Blessed are those who hunger and thirst for righteousness, for they shall be satisfied.
   Blessed are the merciful, for they shall receive mercy.
   Blessed are the pure in heart, for they shall see God.
   Blessed are the peacemakers, for they shall be called sons of God.
   Blessed are those who are persecuted for righteousness' sake, for theirs is the kingdom of heaven.
   Blessed are you when others revile you and persecute you and utter all kinds of evil against you falsely on my account.
   —Matthew 5:3-11

2. Let us not wallow in the valley of despair. I say to you today, my friends, that in spite of the difficulties and frustrations of the moment, I still have a dream. It is a dream deeply rooted in the American dream. I have a dream that one day this nation will rise up and live out the true meaning of its creed: "We hold these truths to be self-evident: that all men are created equal." I have a dream that one day on the red hills of Georgia the sons of former slaves and the sons of former slave owners will be able to sit down together at a table of brotherhood. I have a dream that one day even the state of Mississippi, a state, sweltering with the heat of injustice, sweltering with the heat of oppression, will be transformed into an oasis of freedom and justice. I have a dream that my four little children will one day live in a nation where they will not be judged by the color of their skin but by the content of their character. I have a dream today.
   —Dr. Martin Luther King Jr.

II. Writing Anaphora

A. A Family Vacation (inspired by Charles Dickens)
Write a description of a memorable family vacation using the pattern from the opening lines of *Tale of Two Cities.*

It was _____ ;
   it was _____ .

It was _____ ;
   it was _____ .

It was _____ ;
   it was _____ .

It was _____ ;
   it was _____ .

B. Childhood remembrances (inspired by Joe Brainard)
Write a description of childhood memories using the following pattern. Be sure to include specific images and actions to bring your memory alive for your reader.

Example: I remember trips to the farm and the flip-floppy feeling in my stomach when we drove up the steep hill to the gate.

I remember _____
_____ .

I remember _____
_____ .

I remember _____
_____ .

I remember _____
_____ .

LESSON 20

epistrophe
eh-PIS-truh-fee

From Greek
epi, "upon"
strophe, "a turning"
("wheeling about")

Ending a series of lines, phrases, clauses, or sentences with the same word or words.

> After a great day of sunning and surfing at the beach, I limped back to the car. My clothes were sandy, my hair was sandy, even my teeth were sandy.

Just reading this makes us feel sandy! The repeated use of the adjective *sandy* at the end of each phrase emphasizes the amount of the stuff about to be deposited in the car.

Epistrophe is the opposite of anaphora. The repeated word or words come at the end of each line, phrase, clause, or sentence. The effect, however, is similar. Like anaphora, epistrophe provides dramatic or poetic emphasis to the repeated word or words. The emphasis and rhythm of the repeated words makes them memorable.

In every day speech, anaphora and epistrophe might sound stuffy or inefficient. We see these devices more in poetry and formal speaking. Compare the following examples with and without epistrophe:

With epistrophe:

When I was a child, I spoke like a child, I thought like a child, I reasoned like a child.
—1 Corinthians 13:11

Without epistrophe:

When I was a child, I spoke, thought, and reasoned like a child.

With epistrophe:

...and that government of the people, by the people, for the people shall not perish from the earth.
—Abraham Lincoln, Gettysburg Address

Without epistrophe:

...and that government of, by, and for the people shall not perish from the earth.

These famous lines are less powerful without the rhythm and emphasis of epistrophe. They sound plain and mundane, stripped of the emotional power of the original words.

Use epistrophe to separate a group of ideas into distinct thought-packages, related by structure but each with its own contribution to your overall argument. Two or three repetitions are most common. More than three repetitions (or repeating too many words) can make your reader tired.

Addendum

The rhetorical device called **symploce** (SIM-plo-ke) combines anaphora and epistrophe by repeating words at both the beginning and ending of phrases, clauses, or sentences, as in this example:

It is not enough for the professional to practice tennis; the professional must love tennis.

Unlike anaphora and epistrophe, which emphasize the repeated words, symploce actually focuses our attention on the different words in between the repeated words. By changing only one element of the repeated phrase, we are shining a spotlight on that element. In this example, for instance, you can see that the words *practice* and *love* stand apart from the rest of the sentence.

Lesson 20: Epistrophe

I. Appreciating Epistrophe

A. Underline the repeated words or phrases in the following examples. What is the effect of the epistrophe?

1. But to all of those who would be tempted by weakness, let us leave no doubt that we will be as strong as we need to be for as long as we need to be.
   —Richard Nixon

2. Men have never been good, they are not good, they never will be good.
   —Karl Barth

3. "I'll have my bond!
   Speak not against my bond!
   I have sworn an oath that I will have my bond!"
   —Shylock in William Shakespeare, *Merchant of Venice*, Act 3, Scene 3

4. That which we are, we are.
   —Alfred, Lord Tennyson, "Ulysses"

5. ... you can't sing the blues if you haven't had the blues.
   —David Mamet

II. Writing Epistrophe

A. Rewrite the following sentences using epistrophe by repeating the underlined words.

1. The tournament was a great success due to the time, talents, and energy <u>of many volunteers</u>.

2. After cleaning out the garage his arms, legs, and head <u>ached</u>.

3. I need to find a job: buying food, clothes, and gas <u>takes money</u>.

B. Complete the following sentences using epistrophe by supplying the repeated words.

1. Finishing my homework _____,
   cleaning my room _____,
   and washing the dog _____.

2. Playing video games _____,
   hanging out with friends _____,
   and going to the beach _____.

3. My books _____,
   my music _____,
   my friends _____.

LESSON 21

anadiplosis

an-uh-di-PLOH-sis

From Greek
ana "back"
diploun "to double"

Repeating in the first part of a clause or sentence a prominent word from the latter part of the preceding clause or sentence.

Every evening after dinner Oliver runs basketball drills, drills that he hopes will give him a spot on the varsity team.

Do you get the idea that this aspiring hoopster takes his practice time seriously? That's the result of the repetition of the word "drills" at the end of the first clause and the beginning of the second clause. The repetition emphasizes the main point of the sentence—drills.

Take a look at this example:

> **Everything that can be said, can be said clearly.**
> —Ludwig Wittgenstein

Wittgenstein is actually saying, "Everything can be said clearly." By breaking that thought into two parts he forces you to think about things that "can be said" two times, and in two slightly different contexts. His use of anadiplosis makes his sentence emphatic and memorable.

An anadiplosis that includes a series of repetitions highlights a logical progression of thought, as in this famous example of anadiplosis:

> **Fear leads to anger. Anger leads to hate. Hate leads to suffering.**
> —Yoda, *Star Wars*

A series of repetitions often includes climax, and the two devices together create a chain of thought that stretches to the final conclusion as in this example from the New Testament:

> For this very reason, make every effort to supplement your faith with virtue, and virtue with knowledge, and knowledge with self-control, and self-control with steadfastness, and steadfastness with godliness, and godliness with brotherly affection, and brotherly affection with love.
> —2 Peter 1:5-7

Likewise an anadiplosis with several repetitions can lend an elegant rhythm to your writing, as in this example:

> **The general who became a slave. The slave who became a gladiator. The gladiator who defied an emperor.**
> —Commodus, *Gladiator*

Use anadiplosis to focus your reader's attention on what you think is important, to emphasize a logical progression of thought, and to beautify your writing.

Lesson 21: Anadiplosis | 97

I. Appreciating Anadiplosis

A. Underline the repeated words or phrases in the following examples. What is the effect of the anadiplosis?

1. As soon as the bell was struck it gave out a note, a sweet note such as you might have expected, and not very loud.
   —C.S. Lewis, *The Magician's Nephew*

2. "Aboard my ship, excellent performance is standard. Standard performance is sub-standard. Sub-standard performance is not permitted to exist."
   —Captain Queeg in Herman Wouk, *The Caine Mutiny*

3. More than that, we rejoice in our sufferings, knowing that suffering produces endurance, and endurance produces character, and character produces hope, and hope does not put us to shame, because God's love has been poured into our hearts through the Holy Spirit who has been given to us.
   —Romans 5:3-5

4. "The love of wicked men converts to fear, that fear to hate, and hate turns one or both to worthy danger and deserved death."
   —King Richard in William Shakespeare, *Richard II*, Act 5, Scene 1

II. Writing Anadiplosis

A. Rewrite the following sentences using anadiplosis by replacing the pronouns with the underlined word.

1. I relish good <u>books</u>. They introduce me to endless adventures and fascinating personalities.

2. Diligent practice leads to <u>good technique</u>. It leads to <u>success</u>. It leads to enjoyment.

B. Complete the following sentences using anadiplosis by supplying the repeated words.

1. The key to success in any endeavor is _____.
   _____ not only sets us on the right road but makes sure we arrive at our destination.

2. I want to have _____, but _____ requires _____, and _____ requires _____.

3. Studying leads to _____;
   _____ leads to _____;
   _____ leads to _____.

LESSON 22

"Hard work is the only thing that brings success—just good old-fashioned hard work," Oliver's dad explained.

Nothing unclear about that opinion! The repetition at the end hammers home the first words of sentence. The beginning and end are the positions of emphasis in any sentence, so repeating the same words in both positions doubly emphasizes them.

Sometimes writers use epanalepsis to give deeper meaning to the repeated words, as in the following examples:

> **Next time there won't be a next time.**
> —Phil Leotardo, *The Sopranos*

> **Our eyes saw it, but we could not believe our eyes.**

You find more epanalepsis in poetry than in prose. It conveys strong emotion and a sense of rhythm and balance:

> **Blood hath bought blood,**
> **and blows have answer'd blows;**
> **Strength match'd with strength, and**
> **power confronted power."**
> —Citizen in William Shakespeare,
> *King John*, Act 2 Scene 1

When used successfully in prose, epanalepsis often creates proverb-like sayings (aphorisms) like:

> **Common sense is not so common.**

epanalepsis

ep-uh-nuh-LEP-sis

From Greek
ep, "in addition,"
ana, "back,"
lepsis, "a taking"

Repeating the same word or words at the beginning and end of a clause or sentence.

The length of the clause or sentence between the repeated words can be short:

Success breeds success.

Or long:

In times like these, it is helpful to remember that there have always been times like these.
—Paul Harvey

Use epanalepsis to make your insight sound snappy and stay in your reader's head. When you use this device your thought returns to the place it left, beginning and ending with the same words, but along the way you've deepened the sense of what those words mean.

Lesson 22: Epanalepsis | 101

I. Appreciating Epanalepsis

A. Underline the repeated words or phrases in the following examples. What is the effect of the epanalepsis?

1. "Mankind must put an end to war — or war will put an end to mankind."
   —John F. Kennedy, Speech to UN General Assembly, Sept. 25, 1961

2. Rejoice in the Lord always: again I will say, Rejoice."
   —Philippians 4:4

3. Be all that you can be.
   —U.S. Army Slogan

4. The king is dead; long live the king!

5. "A horse! a horse! my kingdom for a horse!"
   —King Richard in William Shakespeare, *Richard III*, Act 5 Scene 4

6. "Control, control, you must learn control."
   —Yoda in *The Empire Strikes Back*

II. Writing Epanalepsis

A. **Rewrite the following sentences using epanalepsis by repeating the underlined words at the beginning and at the end (you may need to reword the sentences).**

1. The <u>coach</u> calls the shots, so listen to him.

2. <u>Texting</u> may not be your favorite means of communication, but it's the best way to reach me.

3. <u>Practice</u> is tedious, but it's the best way to success.

B. **Complete the following sentences using epanalepsis by supplying the repeated words.**

1. Believe _____,

    _____ believe.

2. Always _____,

    _____ always.

3. Homework _____,

    _____ homework.

LESSON 23

I. Identifying Rhetorical Devices

A. Match the rhetorical devices to their definitions.

1. Joining together two opposing ideas:
   _____

2. Repeating a word or words at the beginning of successive clauses, sentences, or lines:
   _____

3. Using the same pattern of words to present multiple ideas of equal importance:
   _____

4. Ending a series of lines, phrases, clauses, or sentences with the same word or words:
   _____

5. Repeating grammatical structures in inverted order:
   _____

6. Repeating in the first part of a clause or sentence a prominent word from the latter part of the preceding clause or sentence:
   _____

7. Repeating the same word or words at the beginning and end of a clause or sentence:
   _____

Review

Anadiplosis
Anaphora
Antithesis
Chiasmus
Epanelepsis
Epistrophe
Parallelism

II. Recognizing Rhetorical Devices

A. Identify the devices of balance and restatement used in the following examples. Each example may contain more than one device.

1. I am Sam, Sam I am.
   —Dr. Seuss, Green Eggs and Ham

2. If a man will begin with certainties, he shall end in doubts; but if he will be content to begin with doubts he shall end in certainties.
   —Sir Francis Bacon

3. But as for me, my feet had almost stumbled,
   my steps had nearly slipped.
   —Psalm 73:2

4. The years to come seemed waste of breath,
   waste of breath the years behind.
   —William Butler Yeats, "An Irish Airman Foresees his Death"

5. The more we do, the more we can do.
   —William Hazlitt

6. But many who are first will be last, and the last first.
   —Matthew 19:30

B. **Identify the rhetorical devices used in the following examples.**

1. If anyone comes to me and does not hate his own father and mother and wife and children and brothers and sisters, yes, and even his own life, he cannot be my disciple.
   —Luke 14:26

2. For we do not wrestle against flesh and blood . . .
   —Ephesians 6:12a

3. To strive, to seek, to find, and not to yield.
   —Alfred, Lord Tennyson, "Ulysses"

4. This is no minor matter.

5. Believe not all you can hear, tell not all you believe.
   —Native American proverb

6. Dogs, undistinguishable in mire. Horses, scarcely better; splashed to their very blinkers. Foot passengers, jostling one another's umbrellas in a general infection of ill-temper . . .
   —Charles Dickens, *Bleak House*

7. I was not born in a manger. I was actually born on Krypton and sent here by my father, Jor-El, to save the Planet Earth.
   —Senator Barack Obama joking at the Al Smith Dinner

C. Underline and identify the rhetorical devices used by Abraham Lincoln in the Gettysburg Address.

Four score and seven years ago our fathers brought forth on this continent a new nation conceived in Liberty and dedicated to the proposition that all men are created equal.

Now we are engaged in a great civil war, testing whether that nation, or any nation so conceived and so dedicated, can long endure. We are met on a great battle-field of that war. We have come to dedicate a portion of that field as a final resting place for those who here gave their lives that that nation might live. It is altogether fitting and proper that we should do this.

But, in a larger sense, we can not dedicate, we can not consecrate, we can not hallow this ground. The brave men, living and dead, who struggled here, have consecrated it, far above our poor power to add or detract. The world will little note, nor long remember what we say here, but it can never forget what they did here. It is for us the living, rather, to be dedicated here to the unfinished work which they who fought here have thus far so nobly advanced. It is rather for us to be here dedicated to the great task remaining before us — that from these honored dead we take increased devotion to that cause for which they gave the last full measure of devotion — that we here highly resolve that these dead shall not have died in vain — that this nation, under God, shall have a new birth of freedom — and that government of the people, by the people, for the people, shall not perish from the earth.

Devices of Decoration & Variety

LESSON 24

ellipsis

ee-LIP-sis
From Greek
"a leaving out"

Deliberate omission of a word or short phrase which is implied by the context.

In the Penn household, choosing a restaurant is a challenge: Dad votes for Indian cuisine, Mom for Italian, and the kids for sushi.

That sentence doesn't waste any words, does it? No use repeating the word *votes* each time. The context of the sentence implies the omitted words, and the meaning is clear without them.

Why would we want to leave out these words? For one thing, it creates a sense of brevity and conciseness. Notice the matter-of-fact-tone of this example:

> Some people go to priests; others to poetry; I to my friends.
> —Virginia Woolf

At other times omitting words adds force to our sentences as in this example:

> Prosperity is a great teacher; adversity a greater.
> —William Hazlitt

The tight, controlled tone of this statement, with the word *teacher* omitted in the second phrase, emphasizes the remaining words in the sentence and focuses our attention on the antithesis between prosperity and adversity.

While these uses of ellipsis are deliberate and purposeful, the most common examples of ellipsis are often unintentional like these examples:

> While [I was] cleaning my room last week, I discovered some overdue library books.

Though [we were] disappointed that the rain kept us from the beach, we enjoyed playing board games indoors.

Some idiomatic expressions are examples of ellipsis that have become commonplace, like these:

Told you so. (*I* told you so.)
Sounds fine to me. (*It* sounds fine to me.)
Want some? (*Do you* want some?)
Serves you right. (*It* serves you right.)

Ellipsis must be used with care because it is easy to make mistakes like these:

The dog was missing and her owners dejected.

In this example, the missing word *was* is single and does not agree with the plural subject at the end of the sentence. The implied meaning would be grammatically incorrect (... her owners was dejected.)

No teacher has or can expect us to finish so much homework in one night.

Here, the omitted word is *expect*, but that form won't work at the beginning of the sentence (No teacher has expect ...).

Use ellipses for brevity, to make an expression more forceful, or simply as an idiom, but use them with care. The omitted word or phrase must "work" in the place from which it is omitted.

I. Appreciating Ellipsis

A. Explain the following examples of ellipsis. What word is left out? What part of speech is the omitted word?

1. Home — the place where our stomachs get three square meals a day and our hearts, a thousand.

2. The good ended happily, and the bad unhappily. That is what fiction means.
   — Oscar Wilde

3. A good name is better than precious ointment,
   and the day of death than the day of birth.
   — Ecclesiastes 7:1

4. Reading maketh a full man, conference a ready man, and writing an exact man.
   — Francis Bacon, *Of Studies*

5. The man with the average mentality, but with control; with a definite goal, and a clear conception of how it can be gained, and above all, with the power of application and labor, wins in the end."
   — William H. Taft

6. "I'll give my jewels for a set of beads,
   My gorgeous palace for a hermitage,
   My gay apparel for an almsman's gown,
   My figured goblets for a dish of wood . . . ."
   — King Richard in William Shakespeare, *Richard II*, Act 3, Scene 3

II. Writing Ellipsis

A. Cross out the words that could be omitted in an ellipsis.

1. Oliver is the better shooter; Gabe is the better passer.

2. Charlotte has a knack for cooking; Oliver has a knack for eating.

3. A friend who will listen and sympathize, a friend who will be honest and direct, and, most importantly, a friend who will be unwaveringly loyal is a rare treasure.

B. Complete these sentences using ellipsis.

1. The first day of our vacation was _____,

   the second, _____.

2. Some people shop because _____,

   others, because _____.

3. The mall attracts _____,

   the discount store, _____.

4. _____ deal with _____,

   _____, with _____.

LESSON 25

Charlotte had attracted a large crowd as she spoke passionately in front of the library. "Will hardworking students continue to be subjected to homework forever?" she asked as the crowd nodded appreciatively.

We know this rhetorical device called *erotema* as the rhetorical question: when you ask a question but don't expect an answer. A rhetorical question should cause the listener to stop and think about the obvious answer in a way that leads him to agree with the speaker. Charlotte didn't expect the crowd to answer the question, and she didn't either. The answer was obvious: No!

Rhetorical questions serve a variety of purposes. Most often they simply disguise an assertion as in this example:

> **Do we want to spend every waking moment doing homework?**

This rhetorical question really means, "We don't want to spend every waking moment doing homework!"

> **Do we want to have time to pursue other interests and hobbies?**

This example really means, "We want to have time to pursue other interests and hobbies!"

If we ask these questions in rapid succession, we might hope our listeners will get in the habit of agreeing with us and continue to do so as we lay out our argument.

erotema

er-OT-uh-ma

Greek
"question"

Asking a question for effect, rather than to elicit an answer.

Should we sign a petition to outlaw homework?

A final question like this one really means that we should, especially if we've already agreed on the answers to the previous questions.

Not every rhetorical question, however, is a yes or no question.

What has he ever done for me?

This question does not expect a list. The expected answer is obviously *nothing*. The question is a way of denying what it asks.

Sometimes we use rhetorical questions to provoke thought and discussion:

How much homework can we finish in a week?

This question does not expect an objective, measurable answer, but is probably offered only to stimulate a discussion.

Rhetorical questions can even be used sarcastically:

Research shows that homework improves understanding of the subject material. Who knew?

This question really means that everyone knew, because the preceding statement was completely obvious!

The rhetorical question is a powerfully persuasive device—often more persuasive than a direct statement would be. Use rhetorical questions carefully to encourage your listeners or readers to think along with you, but don't use them in a manipulative way or you will lose credibility with your audience.

I. Appreciating Erotema

A. Explain the implied answers to these examples of erotema.

1. Aren't you glad you use Dial? Don't you wish everybody did?"
   —1960s television advertisement for Dial soap

2. How many roads must a man walk down/Before you call him a man?
   —Bob Dylan, "Blowin' in the Wind"

3. What is man that you are mindful of him, and the son of man that you care for him?
   —Psalm 8:4

4. For the great day of their wrath has come, and who can stand it?
   —Revelation 6:17

5. "Here was a Caesar! When comes such another?"
   —Marc Antony in William Shakespeare, *Julius Caesar*, Act 3 Scene 2

6. "Hath not a Jew eyes?
   Hath not a Jew hands, organs, dimensions, senses, affections, passions?
   If you prick us, do we not bleed, if you tickle us, do we not laugh?
   If you poison us, do we not die?"
   —Shylock in William Shakespeare, *Merchant of Venice*, Act 3 Scene 1

II. Writing Erotema

A. Change these statements into rhetorical questions.

1. This essay is not really your best work.

2. There is nothing more fun than a day at the beach.

B. Write a persuasive rhetorical questions for each of these topics.

1. Vote for me to be student body president.

2. Dogs are wonderful pets.

3. Education is the key to success.

LESSON 26

alliteration

uh-lit-uh-REY-shun

from Latin
ad- "to"
littera "letter"

Repeating the same consonant sounds at the beginning of successive or related words.

The group of giggly girls gathered to gawk at the gangly grasshoppers.

While this extremely excessive example is a bit silly, it does illustrate alliteration, which repeats the same sound (not necessarily the same letter) at the beginning of successive words. Alliteration creates a comic effect that will amuse your reader, which is why we often find alliteration in humorous stories.

On the more serious side, poets use alliteration to add rhythm and music to their poetry, as in this example:

> **And sings a solitary song
> That whistles in the wind.**
> —William Wordsworth, "Lucy Gray"

For Anglo-Saxon poetry like *Beowulf* and for early English verse, alliteration was not just a nice flourish—it was the basic structure of the poetry. Alliteration helped a story teller, called a scop, to remember the long stories we call epic poems. Here's an example from *Beowulf*:

> **Girt with God's anger, Grendel came
> gliding
> over the moors beneath misty mounds.**
> —*Beowulf*

Although this type of alliterative verse does not rhyme, the repeated sounds become embedded in memory. This is because patterns help our brains retain and recall information. Alliteration enhances the rhythm of the lines, making the phrases more memorable.

Beginning a group of words with the same sound is effective in prose as well as poetry. It's no coincidence that many common phrases are alliterative, such as:

safe and sound	thick and thin	fair or foul
spick and span	busy as a bee	dead as a doornail

Companies often roll out memorable brand names using alliteration:

Dunkin' Donuts®	Best Buy®	Coca-Cola®
American Airlines®	Krispy Kreme®	Bed, Bath, & Beyond®

Alliteration is commonly used in newspaper headlines that are intended to be memorable, like these examples:

Weather Worries   Drenched by Downpours   Caught on Camera

While it is most common for alliterated words to be next to or close to each other, alliterated words can also be separated if they are related in another way, such as antithesis or parallelism.

When Beau spotted the squirrel, he changed from a model of canine obedience to a mirror of catastrophic obstinacy.

If you're still not sold on the power of alliteration, compare the following phrases and see if you don't agree that alliteration just adds a certain music to our words.

time journey	or	time travel
stuck in a pile	or	stuck in a stack
daily journal	or	daily diary
came to a stop	or	skidded to a stop

A well written alliteration can add sparkle, set a mood, emphasize a thought, or add humor to your speaking and writing.

I. Appreciating Alliteration

A. Underline the alliterative words.

1. cake, kite, knight, sight, canary

2. city, sorry, cake, sister, cynical

3. pneumonia, knight, night, knew, mnemonic

B. Underline the alliterative words in the following examples.

1. Whisper words of wisdom, let it be.
   —The Beatles, "Let It Be"

2. Don't drink and drive.

3. I have stood still and stopped the sound of feet
   When far away an interrupted cry
   Came over houses from another street.
   —Robert Frost, "Acquainted With the Night"

4. Don't dream it. Drive it.
   —Jaguar Advertising Slogan

5. When to the sessions of sweet silent thought
   I summon up remembrance of things past,
   I sigh the lack of many a thing I sought,
   And with old woes new wail my dear times' waste:
   —William Shakespeare, "Sonnet XXX"

6. "These are but wild and whirling words, my lord."
   —Horatio in William Shakespeare, *Hamlet*, Act 1 Scene 5

II. Writing Alliteration

A. Write two alliterative sentences by choosing a word from each column.

Adjectives	Nouns	Verbs
silly	silk	survives
singular	sense	sings
sensible	snail	sinks
sizeable	spaghetti	sips
second-hand	snake	senses

1. _____.

2. _____.

B. Finish the following sentences with alliterative words.

1. Studious students _____.

2. Angry alligators _____.

3. Sizzling steaks _____.

C. Use alliteration to describe the following.

1. A cat or dog

2. A circus

LESSON 27

His quest for wealth was only tilting at windmills.

There's a certain music in this sentence, which contains two examples of assonance: qu*e*st/w*ea*lth and t*i*lting/w*i*ndmills. Both pairs of words share a similar vowel sound in the middle of the word. As in alliteration, the repeated sound is important, not the letter. Notice that the vowel sound must be followed by different consonants. Otherwise, we would have rhyme rather than assonance, as in qu*est*/r*est* or w*ealth*/h*ealth*. You can think of alliteration occurring at the beginning of a word, rhyme occurring at the end, and assonance taking the middle ground.

Each of these three devices of sound are common in poetry, where they add a sense of continuity or fluidity to the lines by linking sounds. Assonance is particularly useful in poetry that does not use a rhyming scheme. It gives the poet great flexibility while still adding a musical quality to the verse.

> "Courage!" he said, and pointed toward the land,
> "This mounting wave will roll us shoreward soon."
> —Alfred, Lord Tennyson, "The Lotus-Eaters"

Even in prose, however, assonance works subtly to create an elegant effect. It may not be as noticeable as alliteration, but assonance can set a tone or mood in a subconscious way. Vowel sounds that are formed by the tongue high in the mouth like short "i" are associated with light elegance and give energy to prose. Vowels sounds formed by the tongue low in

assonance

AS-uh-nuhns

from Latin
ad- "to"
sonare "to sound"

The repetition of similar vowel sounds preceded and followed by different consonants.

the mouth like short "u" and long sounds like long "a" or "oo" slow down prose and give it a more heavy feeling. Compare these examples:

A c<u>i</u>ty set on a h<u>i</u>ll cannot be h<u>i</u>d.
S<u>u</u>dden th<u>u</u>nder caused <u>u</u>s to sh<u>u</u>dder.
I r<u>o</u>se and t<u>o</u>ld him of my w<u>o</u>e.

Usually, assonant words are sprinkled throughout a sentence like the examples above. Sometimes assonance is used for a pair of words next to each other. In fact, many common phrases owe their appeal to assonance:

sweet dreams   high as a kite
hit or miss   mad as a hatter
fancy pants   free as a breeze

Either way, the assonance should fall on the stressed syllables.

In either poetry or prose, use assonance, as well as alliteration, to give a lyrical quality to your words. Listen to the sound of your writing. Try out different synonyms to see which ones produce the most musical sound.

I. Appreciating Assonance

A. Underline the assonant words.

1. lake, weight, brat, braid, cream

2. city, receive, flies, nibble, syllable

3. please, niece, ski, tree, cheap

B. Underline the assonant words in the following examples.

1. It beats as it sweeps as it cleans.
   —Slogan for Hoover vacuum cleaners

2. And the Raven, never flitting, still is sitting, still is sitting.
   —Edgar Allen Poe, "The Raven"

3. Night came on, and a full moon rose high over the trees into the sky lighting the land till it lay bathed in ghostly day.
   —Jack London, *The Call of the Wild*

4. Old age should burn and rave at close of day;
   Rage, rage, against the dying of the light.
   —Dylan Thomas, "Do not go gentle into that good night"

5. Poetry is old, ancient, goes back far. It is among the oldest of living things. So old it is that no man knows how and why the first poems came.
   —Carl Sandburg, "Early Moon"

II. Writing Assonance

A. Write two examples of assonance for each of the following words.

1. cat:

2. mutt:

3. beast:

4. bite:

B. Form each set of assonant words above into a sentence.

1.

2.

3.

4.

C. Use assonance to describe the following.

1. Smile

2. Spring

LESSON 28

Oliver's request to borrow the family car for a trip to the beach was met by thunderous silence.

Silence means no sound, and thunderous means a loud sound, so it really doesn't make much sense to put these words together. When two words that seem contradictory join forces for rhetorical effect, we have an oxymoron. Like enemies who suddenly embrace cooperation, an oxymoron makes us stop and stare. In this case the silence of Oliver's parents speaks louder than words.

Examples of literary oxymorons abound, each with it's own sharp emphasis that makes us consider the relationship of the words and thereby understand a deeper meaning suggested by the contradiction. Think about the surprising truth to these apparent contradictions:

> sweet pain
> thunderous silence
> cruel kindness
> living death
> wise fool
> lonely crowd

These objective oxymorons describe an actual contradiction. A true oxymoron, although appearing to be contradictory, must contain a measure of truth. The truth disguised by the contradiction sneaks up and surprises us.

In popular usage the term oxymoron has come to mean nearly any sort of contradiction. Whether one considers this to be a misunderstanding of the term or not depends on how much of a purist one is!

oxymoron

awk-see-MOHR-on

From Greek
oxys, "sharp"
moros, "dull"

The yoking of two words that seem contradictory but together create a new meaning with surprising truth.

Subjective oxymorons reflect the writer's opinion that the terms are mutually exclusive even though the terms are not inherently contradictory:

internet security
rap music
airline food
affordable housing

Other similar examples are simply meant to be funny or cynical:

army intelligence
postal service
responsible government
honest lawyer

Some oxymorons are created accidently, usually in informal conversation:

extremely average
objective opinion
accurate estimate
almost exactly

A fresh and clever oxymoron adds originality and impact to writing. It stops the reader in his tracks and forces him to think about the subject in a new way. The danger of oxymorons is familiarity. They can quickly become stale and lose their impact.

Addendum:
An oxymoron is sometimes called a condensed paradox. Like oxymoron, a paradox is based on apparent contradiction. The contradiction, however, is reflected in an entire statement rather than the pairing of words, as in this example:

Art is a form of lying in order to tell the truth.
—Pablo Picasso

When a paradox is reduced to two words, we call it an oxymoron.

I. Appreciating Oxymoron

A. Underline the contradictory terms in these examples of oxymoron. What surprising truth is revealed?

1. There are some enterprises in which a careful disorderliness is the true method.
   —Herman Melville, *Moby Dick*

2. "I know this is a joyful trouble to you."
   —Macduff in William Shakespeare, *Macbeth*, Act 2 Scene 3

3. I do here make humbly bold to present them with a short account of themselves and their art.....
   —Jonathan Swift, *A Tale of a Tub*

4. O miserable abundance, O beggarly riches!
   —John Donne, *Devotions Upon Emergent Occasions*

5. "O brawling love! O loving hate! . . .
   O heavy lightness! serious vanity!
   Misshapen chaos of well-seeming forms!
   Feather of lead, bright smoke, cold fire, sick health!
   Still-waking sleep, that is not what it is!
   This love feel I, that feel no love in this."
   —Romeo in William Shakespeare, *Romeo and Juliet*, Act 1 Scene 1

II. Writing Oxymorons

A. Choose an adjective from the first list and a noun from the second list to make an oxymoron, or make up your own oxymoron with an adjective/noun pattern.

Positive Adjectives: peaceful, generous, harmonious, abundant
Negative Nouns: conflict, need, disagreement, poverty, lack, discord

1. _____ 2. _____

Negative Adjectives: disagreeable, horrid, stingy, deceitful
Positive Nouns: charity, peace, generosity, harmony, honesty

3. _____ 4. _____

B. Choose an adverb from the first list and an adjective from the second list to make an oxymoron, or make up your own oxymoron with an adverb/adjective pattern.

Positive Adverbs: happily, cheerfully, fabulously, festively
Negative Adjectives: horrible, impoverished, depressed, filthy

1. _____ 2. _____

Negative Adverbs: lazily, greedily, miserably, shamefully
Positive Adjectives: blissful, wealthy, thoughtful, sunny

3. _____ 4. _____

C. Choose an noun from the first list and a verb from the second list to make an oxymoron, or make up your own oxymoron with an noun/verb pattern.

Nouns: silence, sleep, whisper
Verbs: sings, whistles, shouts, screams

1. _____ 2. _____

LESSON 29

Our night in the peaceful outdoors was marred by buzzing mosquitoes and a whirring generator.

Because it is difficult to describe sounds, we choose words that sound like sounds to make our writing more lively and interesting. These words are called onomatopoeia.

Notice that many examples of onomatopoeia do not replicate exactly the sounds they describe. Often the resemblance is one of convention rather than reality. Sometimes it is only a syllable that imitates the sound. Nevertheless, onomatopoeia does help us to appreciate the full flavor of words.

The most common examples of onomatopoeia include animal sounds like:

oink	meow	roar	neigh
croak	quack	bark	hiss
chirp	cluck	purr	cuckoo

human sounds like:

burp	chomp	whine	crunch
gulp	cough	hum	boo hoo
gasp	moan	babble	whisper

and nature sounds like:

whoosh	swish	sigh	drip
trickle	gurgle	splash	flutter

Others describe the sounds of machines:

chug	creak	honk	ka-ching
crash	squeak	whir	click-clack

onomatopoeia

on-uh-mat-uh-PEE-uh

from Greek
onomos, "name"
poiein, "to make"

A word that imitates the sound it describes.

and alarms:

| buzz | beep | tweet | bong | clang |

and, of course, fighting:

| pow | bif | bam | thump | smash |
| zowie | whomp | bang | | |

Using onomatopoeia adds interesting sounds that enliven our writing. Compare these phrases:

crying babies	or	squawking babies
frying bacon	or	sizzling bacon
the sound of wind	or	the murmur of wind
the noise of a clunker	or	the rattle of a clunker

In addition to the lively quality produced by onomatopoeia, poets often use more subtle forms of this device in order to convey the meaning of their verse.

Compare the long, slow sounds of Tennyson's lines to the harsh, unpleasant sounds in Browning's lines:

> Here are cool mosses deep,
> And through the moss the ivies creep,
> And in the stream the long-leaved flowers weep,
> And from the craggy ledge the poppy hangs in sleep.
> —Alfred, Lord Tennyson, "Song of the Lotus-Eaters"

> A tap at the pane,
> the quick sharp scratch
> And blue spurt of a lighted match.
> —Robert Browning, "Meeting at Night"

Use onomatopoeia to match the sound of words with their sense. Some sounds are soft and soothing, light and happy. Others are angry or chaotic, dark or gloomy. Choose words which match your intent, and your writing will be more musical and descriptive.

I. Appreciating Onomatopoeia

A. Underline the examples of onomatopoeia in these lines from stanza three of Edgar Allan Poe's poem called "The Bells."

Hear the loud alarm bells—
Brazen bells!
What a tale of terror, now, their turbulency tells!
In the startled ear of night
How they scream out their affright!
Too much horrified to speak,
They can only shriek, shriek,
Out of tune,
In a clamorous appealing to the mercy of the fire,
In a mad expostulation with the deaf and frantic fire,
Leaping higher, higher, higher,
With a desperate desire,
And a resolute endeavor,
Now—now to sit or never,
By the side of the pale-faced moon.
Oh, the bells, bells, bells!
What a tale their terror tells
Of Despair!
How they clang, and clash, and roar!
What a horror they outpour
On the bosom of the palpitating air!
Yet the ear it fully knows,
By the twanging,
And the clanging,
How the danger ebbs and flows:
Yet the ear distinctly tells,
In the jangling,
And the wrangling,
How the danger sinks and swells,
By the sinking or the swelling in the anger of the bells—
Of the bells—
Of the bells, bells, bells, bells,
Bells, bells, bells—
In the clamor and the clangor of the bells!

II. Writing Onomatopoeia

A. Write two examples of onomatopoeia for each of the following sounds.

1. explosion:

2. alarm clock:

3. laughter:

4. engine:

B. Use onomatopoeia from the list above to write four sentences.

1.

2.

3.

4.

C. Write a free verse poem using onomatopoeia to describe cooking breakfast.

Making Breakfast on a Saturday Morning

_____

_____

_____

_____

LESSON 30

I. Identifying Rhetorical Devices

A. Match the rhetorical devices to their definitions.

1. The repetition of similar vowel sounds preceded and followed by different consonants:

   _____

2. Asking a question for effect, rather than to elicit an answer:

   _____

3. A word that imitates the sound it describes:

   _____

4. Repeating the same sounds at the beginning of successive or related words:

   _____

5. The yoking of two words that seem contradictory but together create a new meaning with surprising truth:

   _____

6. Deliberate omission of a word or short phrase which is implied by the context:

   _____

Review

Alliteration
Assonance
Ellipsis
Erotema
Onomatopoeia
Oxymoron

II. Recognizing Rhetorical Devices

A. Identify the devices of decoration and variety used in the following examples.

1. The soul selects her own society.
   —Emily Dickinson, "The soul selects her own society"

2. Hear the mellow wedding bells.
   —Edgar Allan Poe, "Bells"

3. What is so rare as a day in June?
   —James Russell Lowell, "The Vision of Sir Launfal"

4. The world is a comedy to those who think, a tragedy to those who feel.
   —Horace Walpole

5. The crumbling thunder of seas...
   —Robert Louis Stevenson, "The Feast of Famine"

6. That building is a little bit big and pretty ugly.
   —James Thurber

B. Identify the rhetorical devices used in the following examples.

1. A Brother may not be a Friend, but a Friend will always be a Brother.
   — Benjamin Franklin

2. A house without a woman and firelight, is like a body without soul or sprite.
   — Benjamin Franklin

3. The wise Man draws more advantage from his Enemies, than the Fool from his Friends.
   — Benjamin Franklin

4. Be not niggardly of what costs thee nothing, as courtesy, counsel, and countenance.
   — Benjamin Franklin

5. I pray Heav'n defend these Colonies from every enemy; and give them bread enough, peace enough, money enough, and plenty of good cyder.
   — Benjamin Franklin

6. He that's content hath much. He that complains has too much.
   — Benjamin Franklin

7. Sudden Pow'r is apt to be insolent, sudden Liberty saucy; that behaves best which has grown gradually.
   — Benjamin Franklin

8. Nothing brings more Pain than too much Pleasure; nothing more bondage than too much Liberty.
   — Benjamin Franklin

C. **Underline and identify the rhetorical devices used by Edgar Allen Poe in this passage from "The Raven."**

Once upon a midnight dreary, while I pondered, weak and weary,	1
Over many a quaint and curious volume of forgotten lore—	2
While I nodded, nearly napping, suddenly there came a tapping,	3
As of some one gently rapping, rapping at my chamber door.	4
"'Tis some visitor," I muttered, "tapping at my chamber door—	5
Only this and nothing more."	6
Ah, distinctly I remember it was in the bleak December,	7
And each separate dying ember wrought its ghost upon the floor.	8
Eagerly I wished the morrow;—vainly I had sought to borrow	9
From my books surcease of sorrow—sorrow for the lost Lenore—	10
For the rare and radiant maiden whom the angels name Lenore—	11
Nameless here for evermore.	12
And the silken sad uncertain rustling of each purple curtain	13
Thrilled me—filled me with fantastic terrors never felt before;	14
So that now, to still the beating of my heart, I stood repeating	15
"'Tis some visitor entreating entrance at my chamber door—	16
Some late visitor entreating entrance at my chamber door;	17
This it is and nothing more."	18

APPENDICES

APPENDIX A

Rhetorical Devices in Context

In the first-century A.D., a rhetorician named Quintilianus published *Institutes of Oratory*, which set forth five "cannons," or parts, to the study of rhetoric. Here are the Five Cannons of Rhetoric he discussed:

Inventio (Invention)	*Dispositio* (Arrangement)	*Elocutio* (Style)	*Memoria* (Memorization)	*Pronuntiatio* (Delivery)
Method for discovering arguments.	Method for selecting and organizing arguments.	Choice and arrangement of words including: correctness, clearness, appropriateness, and ornament. Ornament includes the use of rhetorical devices.	Recalling arguments, specifically, creating structures that would aid in memory.	Skill in delivering arguments.

When we study rhetorical devices, we're concerned with the Style Canon. After we've discovered and arranged the proofs for an argument, we want to present them in a way that is correct, clear, appropriate, and beautiful. Correctness includes proper grammar and word usage. Clearness means that we choose words that illuminate rather than obscure our meaning. In addition, our words should be appropriate, or fitting, to the situation. Finally, we hope to express our thoughts with style. In the context of rhetoric, style most often refers to figures of speech: changing the ordinary pattern or arrangement of words or the ordinary meaning of words. These figures, also called rhetorical devices, are only a sliver of the study of rhetoric—the tip of the iceberg.

Today, whether you are studying classical rhetoric in a rhetoric class or simply trying to structure and deliver your thoughts in the best way possible, it's valuable to know a little about this time-honored discipline.

If you would like to know more about the history of rhetoric, the other canons of rhetoric, or rhetorical devices, you might be interested in these resources:

"Rhetorical Musings Blog." www.writerstoolbox.net.

> Rhetorical devices are commonplace in everyday speech and writing. In the "Rhetorical Musings Blog" you can read about and contribute examples of rhetorical devices found in everyday life and literature.

Corbett, Edward P.J. *Classical Rhetoric for the Modern Student*. 3rd ed. New York: Oxford University Press, 1990.

> The author begins with a brief explanation of rhetoric in Chapter I. Chapter II covers the discovery of arguments; Chapter III, the arrangement of arguments. Chapter IV deals with style, including rhetorical devices. Chapter V is an extensive survey of the history of rhetoric.

Harris, Robert A. *Writing with Clarity and Style: A Guide to Rhetorical Devices for Contemporary Writers*. Los Angeles: Pyrczak Publishing, 2003.

> The author uses contemporary examples to explain the use of sixty rhetorical devices. The Appendices include examples of common communication with and without rhetorical devices, including a newspaper editorial, business memorandum, social worker's report about a client, graduate school application essay, and a short story. Much of this information is available online at www.virtualsalt.com.

Bluedorn, Nathaniel & Hans. *The Fallacy Detective*. 3rd ed. Muscatine, Iowa: Christian Logic. 2009.

> The authors present logical fallacies in a fun and interesting format.

APPENDIX B

Vocabulary Game

Materials:
- **Vocabulary Cards**
  One device name on each card, one set of cards for each team of 4-6 students. Here's an example:
- **Definition & Example List**
  See Appendix C.
- **Signal Device**
  Bell

> **Hyperbole**

Instructions:
1. Divide students into teams of four to six players.
2. Have each team stand around a table with a bell in the center. Be sure that all students can reach the bell.
3. Give each team a stack of vocabulary cards containing one card for each rhetorical device that the class has studied.
4. Distribute vocabulary cards among the team members. Each team member should be holding one to four cards.
5. Students pass their cards slowly around the circle in one direction.
6. While students are slowly passing cards around the circle, the teacher reads a definition or example of a rhetorical device from the list in Appendix C.
7. The student holding the card with the corresponding term rings the bell.
8. The teacher recognizes the team that has signalled first and asks the student to show the card and identify the term.
9. If the student correctly identifies the term, the team receives a point.
10. If the student incorrectly identifies the term, the other team may identify the definition and receive a point.
11. Play for a specified period of time and then total the points for each team to determine the winner.

Alternatively, students may sit in a circle and pass cards around the circle. The first student to stand may identify the term.

"Question the Answer" Game

Materials:
- **Answer Cards**
  Make Answer Cards with one device name and definition per card. Cards should include the device category (chapter title), as well. Here's an example:
- **Envelopes**
  Take four envelopes and write one device category (chapter title) on each one. Put the Answer Cards into the corresponding envelope so that students can see the name of the category, but not the question or answer.
- **Signal Device**
  Either a bell or some small object that the students can "grab."

> **Devices of Association**
>
> **A:** An explicit comparison of two unlike things, often employing "like" or "as."
>
> **Q:** What is a simile?

Instructions:
1. Divide students into two teams. The first students from each team face each other across a table. Place signal device on the table between the two contestants.
2. Lay out the category envelopes for devices that the class has studied.
3. Teacher takes a card from the envelope for the last category studied and reads the definition of the device.
4. When one of the two contestants recognizes the device, he or she signals. As soon as a student signals, the teacher should stop reading the definition.
5. The first student to signal may ask the question, "What is _____?" and receive a point for his/her team for a correct answer.
6. If the response is incorrect, or if the student does not answer in a question format, finish reading the definition and the opposing player may give the question and receive a point for his/her team.
7. The winning player remains at the table, while the losing player returns to the end of his/her line. The winning player may choose the next category.
8. If neither player knows the correct question, both students return to the end of their lines, and the last team to choose a category chooses again.
9. Play until all cards are gone or for a specified period of time, and then total the points for each team to determine the winner.

APPENDIX C

Chapter and Lesson numbers appear in parenthesis after each definition.

Alliteration: Repeating the same consonant sounds at the beginning of successive or related words. (4-26)

> The group of giggly girls gathered to gawk at the gangly grasshoppers.

Allusion: A short, informal reference to a famous person or event. (1-4)

> Oliver shrugged his heavy backpack onto his shoulders and trudged off to class, looking like Atlas himself.

Anadiplosis: Repeating in the first part of a clause or sentence a prominent word from the latter part of the preceding clause or sentence. (3-21)

> Every evening after dinner Oliver runs basketball drills, drills that he hopes will give him a spot on the varsity team.

Anaphora: Repeating a word or words at the beginning of successive clauses, sentences, or lines. (3-19)

> Mom finally agreed to take us to the beach this summer if we cleaned up our rooms, if we mowed the lawn, and if we finished our summer-school reading.

Antithesis: Joining together two opposing ideas. (3-18)

> Charlotte's idea of summer vacation is rest and relaxation; her mother's idea is extra time for chores.

Assonance: The repetition of similar vowel sounds preceded and followed by different consonants. (4-27)

> His quest for wealth was only tilting at windmills.

Asyndeton: Omitting conjunctions between words, phrases, or clauses. (2-9)

> Mr. Penn was a real Renaissance man, excelling in music, art, literature, astronomy, architecture.

Chiasmus: Repeating grammatical structures in inverted order. (3-17)

> This afternoon Charlotte rushed happily to the library, then sadly returned to her chores.

Climax: Arranging ideas expressed in words, phrases or clauses in order of increasing importance. (2-8)

> Our new puppy, Beau, went crazy in my room yesterday. He chewed up three of my pens, a notebook, my favorite pair of sneakers, and my iPod!

Ellipsis: Deliberate omission of a word or short phrase which is implied by the context. (4-24)

> In the Penn household, choosing a restaurant is a challenge: Dad votes for Indian cuisine, Mom for Italian, and the kids for sushi.

Epanalepsis: Repeating the same word or words at the beginning and end of a clause or sentence. (3-22)

> "Hard work is the only thing that brings success—just good old-fashioned hard work," Oliver's dad explained.

Epistrophe: Ending a series of lines, phrases, clauses, or sentences with the same word or words. (3-20)

> After a great day of sunning and surfing at the beach, I limped back to the car. My clothes were sandy, my hair was sandy, even my teeth were sandy.

Erotema: Asking a question for effect, rather than to elicit an answer. (4-25)

> Charlotte had attracted a large crowd as she spoke passionately in front of the library. "Will hard-working students continue to be subjected to homework forever?" she asked as the crowd nodded appreciatively.

Hyperbole: Extravagant exaggeration not intended to be taken literally. (2-14)

> While some dogs may eat you out of house and home, we're more concerned with Beau eating our house and home!

Irony: An incongruity between what might be expected and what actually occurs or is said. (2-11)

> "Well, I don't think my essay is very good," Oliver told his teacher, " but at least it's 200 words shorter than the required word count."

Litotes: Expressing a thought by denying its opposite. (2-13)

> Oliver held up his ruined iPod, not unhappily. "I guess this means I can get the newest model now."

Metaphor: An implied comparison made by referring to one thing as another. (1-2)

> Although she was nervous at the beginning of the gymnastics competition, Charlotte's performance was a rare gem, and she returned home proudly flashing a gold medal.

Metonymy: A reference to an object or concept by using a word closely related to or suggested by the original word. (1-5)

> "As soon as the kettle boils, I'll make you a cup of tea," Charlotte called to her ill mother.

Onomatopoeia: A word that imitates the sound it describes. (4-29)

> Our night in the peaceful outdoors was marred by buzzing mosquitoes and a whirring generator.

Oxymoron: The yoking of two words that seem contradictory but together create a new meaning with surprising truth. (4-28)

> Oliver's request to borrow the family car for a trip to the beach was met by thunderous silence.

Parallelism: Using the same pattern of words to present multiple ideas of equal importance. (3-16)

> Oliver was a pretty normal kid. He usually did his homework, rarely cleaned his room, and never ate his peas.

Personification: Attributing human qualities to something that is not human. (1-3)

> As Oliver raced to finish his homework before leaving for school, the printer choked up and thwarted his best intentions.

Polysyndeton: Using conjunctions between each word, phrase, or clause. (2-10)

> After years of dreaming and thinking and planning and saving and working, Mrs. Penn's dream of becoming a vet became a reality.

Simile: An explicit comparison of two unlike things, often employing "like" or "as." (1-1)

> Oliver had fallen behind on his algebra homework. Now polynomial factoring loomed over his weekend like a dark cloud threatening to spoil the fun.

Synecdoche: A representation of the whole by naming one of its parts, or vice versa. (1-6)

> If you want to spot Oliver at the orchestra concert tomorrow night, just look for the strings.

Understatement: Expressing an idea as less important than it actually is. (2-12)

> Oliver looked at the mess left by our new puppy's chewing spree. "Well, it looks like Beau had a busy day," he said, as Mom held up her favorite (now tattered) sweater.

APPENDIX D

Lesson 1: Simile

I. A. Explain Similes

1. a. How Bilbo feels
   b. Butter scraped over too much bread
   c. The subjects are both too small to be satisfying.

2. a. The Kingdom of Heaven
   b. Treasure hidden in a field
   c. They are both so desirable that they should be sought after at any cost.

3. a. His absence
   b. Winter
   c. Both are dreary.

4. a. The King's favor
   b. Clouds that bring the spring rain
   c. Both are harbingers of good things to come.

5. a. The eagle
   b. A thunderbolt
   c. Both are quick and might have consequences for those in their paths.

6. a. The troops
   b. Bees
   c. Both are active, noisy, potentially dangerous, and in large groups.

Lesson 2: Metaphor

I. A. Explain Metaphors
1. a. The relationship between Christ and the church
   b. A vine with branches
   c. Both are living, and the branches in each case are dependent upon the vine.

2. a. Fog
   b. A little cat
   c. They both move silently when and where they please.

3. a. Happiness
   b. A thin layer of ice
   c. Both can be shattered easily.

4. a. The world
   b. A theatrical performance
   c. Men and women are like actors in that they enter the stage (are born) and exit the stage (die) and play many parts (fill many roles).

B. Mixed Metaphor
1. a. Burning the midnight oil
   b. Burning a candle from both ends
   c. He is working past the end of daylight, when one would normally stop working.

2. a. He's green (new at something).
   b. Wet behind the ears (hasn't matured).
   c. He's inexperienced.

Lesson 3: Personification

I. A. Explain Personification
1. a. Plants
   b. The ability to cry like a baby who needs attention

2. a. Time
   b. The ability to talk and the human need to be right

3. a. The waters
   b. The capability to be afraid and to tremble in fear

4. a. Death
   b. The ability to be proud and strong, and the ability to fight and kill as a person would

Lesson 4: Allusion

I. A. Explain Allusions
1. a. Noah building an ark
   b. Indicates the uselessness of predicting a disaster if you don't do anything about it.

2. a. Hercules, known for his great strength
   b. Hamlet compares himself unfavorably to Hercules and, likewise, his uncle unfavorably to his father.

3. a. In Greek mythology, Scylla and Charybdis were two great dangers on either side of a narrow strait. To pass safely between them was a great feat.
   b. Both plot and plotlessness can prove dangerous for a writer.

4. a. The Greek poet Homer and his epic poems *Iliad* and *Odyssey*
   b. The mosquito's buzz was as descriptive of its wrath and its travels around the room as Homer's poems were of the wrath of Achilles and the wanderings of Odysseus.

Lesson 5: Metonymy

I. A. **Explain Metonymy**
   1. a. "The suits" refers to businessmen and bankers.
      b. Bankers and businessmen must appear professional at all times, so they wear suits, which are used to characterize them.

   2. a. "Redcoats" refer to British soldiers.
      b. British soldiers at the time of the American Revolution wore red coats, which are used to identify them.

   3. a. "Houston" refers to the city where NASA is located.
      b. The name of the city where NASA flight control is located is used to address the flight controllers themselves.

   4. a. "Sweat of your brow" refers to the sweat that pours from your face when you work hard.
      b. The sweat is used to refer to the hard labor that causes it.

   5. a. "Black ink" refers to written words.
      b. The ink used to write poetry is used to refer to the sentiments contained in the words.

Lesson 6: Synecdoche

I. A. **Explain Synecdoche**
   1. a. "New set of wheels" refers to a vehicle.
      b. A part of the car is used to refer to the car itself.

   2. a. "Souls with their bodies" refers to men and women; "roof" refers to a house.
      b. Parts of a person are used to refer to a person, and a part of a house is used to refer to the house.

   3. a. "Face" refers to God.
      b. A (non-literal) part of God's personhood refers to his presence.

   4. a. "Glass" refers to a mirror and "dial" refers to a clock.
      b. A part of each item is used to refer to the item itself.

Appendix D | 151

B. **Metonymy or Synecdoche?**
1. Synecdoche. A part of the groceries (bacon) stands for all the groceries that Dad's income buys.

2. Metonymy. Boots worn by a soldier stand for the soldier himself. The word "ground" might also be a synecdoche for the country that the ground is in.

3. Metonymy. The author Shakespeare stands for his poetry.

4. Synecdoche. A part of a cow (head) stands for the whole cow.

5. Metonymy. The ear stands for the sympathetic listening that it performs.

6. Synecdoche. A part of a person (heart) stands for the person.
OR
Metonymy. The part of a person often associated with the will stands for determination of will.

7. Synecdoche. A part of a person (face) stands for the whole person.

8. Synecdoche. A part of a person (guts) stands for the whole person.

Lesson 7: Review

I. **Identifying Rhetorical Devices**
   A. 1. Personification
      2. Metonymy
      3. Metaphor
      4. Synecdoche
      5. Allusion
      6. Simile

II. Recognizing Rhetorical Devices

A. 1. Personification—wisdom is personified as a woman calling out in the marketplace.

2. Metonymy—a customer is referred to by what he ordered.

3. Synecdoche—one season of the year is used to refer to the entire year; Metaphor—passing years are a besieging army attacking a woman's face and digging trenches across her beauty.

4. Allusion—"Prodigal" refers to the prodigal son in the biblical parable who is reduced by hunger to eating with the pigs.

5. Simile—Thoreau's serenity is like water with only small ripples in it.

6. Metaphor—The political division between eastern and western Europe was an iron curtain that divided them.

B. 1. "Psalm 23"
   a. "The Lord is my shepherd" is a metaphor for God's care for his people.
   b. "Green pastures" is a metaphor for abundant provision.
   c. "Still waters" is a metaphor for safety.
   d. "Paths of righteousness" is a metaphor for obedience.
   e. "Valley of the shadow of death" is a metaphor for death.
   f. "Your rod and your staff" are metaphors for correction and discipline.
   g. "Table" is a metaphor for a feast or a metonymy for God's provision of what is on the table.
   h. "Anoint my head with oil" is a metaphor for a healing balm.
   i. "My cup overflows" is a metaphor for overflowing blessings.
   j. "Goodness and mercy" are personified. They have the ability to follow after.

2. "A Book"
   a. food and drink
   b. wings

Lesson 8: Climax

I. A. Explain Climax
1. a. come to the gate / open the gate / tear down the wall
   b. These ideas build from acknowledging the isolated nature of the Soviet Union and Eastern Europe to actually ending the isolation.

2. a. expressing aspirations / seeking practical plans / translating concept into action
   b. These ideas build from abstract to concrete.

3. a. the Word existed / the Word was with God / the Word was God
   b. These ideas build from existence of Jesus to association of Jesus with God to identification of Jesus as God.

Lesson 9: Asyndeton

I. A. Explain Asyndeton
1. Bubba's list of all the ways you can prepare shrimp sounds like it might be incomplete (even though he says, "That's about it.").

2. Churchill's list of all the places Britain would fight the Nazis sounds like an incomplete list. The point is that there wasn't any place that they wouldn't fight, so the list could go on and on.

3. MacArthur uses two asyndetic lists in this speech to make climax more powerful: "what you ought to be, what you can be, what you will be" and "build courage ... , regain faith ... , create hope."

Lesson 10: Polysyndeton

I. A. Explain Polysyndeton
1. The Magna Carta's polysyndetic list of the rights of free men emphasizes and gives due weight to each right in the list, showing that they are all equal in importance.

2. Isaiah's polysyndetic restating of God's actions slows down the rhythm of the sentence so we can absorb the full meaning of the words.

3. The polysyndetic list of events makes the doom of Meneltarma seem like a piling on of one catastrophic event after another. The polysyndetic list of all the people and things that were destroyed emphasizes that the destruction was total — everything slid into the sea.

Lesson 11: Irony

I. A. Explain Irony
1. a. It would seem that fiction could be stranger than truth.
   b. Twain, however, says that truth is stranger, because sometimes events in real life don't even seem possible.

2. a. It would seem that if you were surrounded by water that having something to drink would be the least of your worries.
   b. Because it was salt water, though, there was not a drop to drink.
   c. Situational irony

3. a. Pilate meant to indicate that Jesus was being crucified because he claimed to be a king in rebellion to Caesar.
   b. The hidden truth is that He is indeed a king, a king over Caesar and all creation.
   c. Dramatic irony

Lesson 12: Understatement

I. A. Explain Understatement
1. a. Twain is alive.
   b. Rather than Twain saying the reports of his death are false, he says they are merely exaggerated.

2. a. Mercutio has a mortal wound.
   b. Rather than saying he is going to die from his wound, Mercutio says the wound is not unusually large.

3. a. Captain Lawrence is going out to die.
   b. Rather than saying that he will not be coming back, Lawrence says he may be gone for some time.

4. a. Watson and Crick's exciting discovery opened up many new areas of inquiry in biology.
   b. Rather than saying that their discovery will make a huge impact on their field, Watson and Crick say it is interesting.

Lesson 13: Litotes

I. A. Explain Litotes
1. a. not many
   b. Only a few of the Christians in the Church at Corinth were worldly wise, powerful, or of noble birth.

2. a. not in this land shall he remain uncaught
   b. In this land, he shall be caught.

3. a. no obscure city
   b. Tarsus is a well-known city.

4. a. not startled; not conscious of a terrible sensation
   b. Scrooge *was* startled and he *was* conscious of a terrible sensation. In this passage, Dickens goes on to deny the litotes itself: It was not true that Scrooge was not startled.

Lesson 14: Hyperbole

I. A. Explain Hyperbole
1. a. "It is easier for a camel to go through the eye of a needle."
   b. It is difficult for a rich man to enter the Kingdom of God.

2. a. "And fired the shot heard round the world."
   b. The news of the battle would spread far and wide.

3. a. "...my hand will rather the multitudinous seas incarnadine..."
   b. Macbeth is guilty of the heinous sin of killing his king and kinsman, and he feels that nothing will wash away his guilt.

Lesson 15: Review

I. Identifying Rhetorical Devices
   A. 1. Understatement
      2. Climax
      3. Polysyndeton
      4. Hyperbole
      5. Irony
      6. Asyndeton
      7. Litotes

II. Recognizing Rhetorical Devices
   A. 1. Polysyndeton—Lewis lists the actions with conjunctions to show the equal importance of each one and give the idea of piling on mishap upon mishap.

   2. Hyperbole—It's so hard to learn German that three of Twain's teachers died while he was trying.

   3. Asyndeton—This list of the fruit that flows from the Spirit gives the impression of an incomplete list that could continue.

   4. Litotes—"No easy bargain" means it will be difficult to come to terms with the guardian of the treasure.

   5. Irony—You would expect that Thoreau would be delighted to see someone coming to do him good, but instead he runs in the other

direction. Perhaps those who think they are going to "do you good" usually don't. Thoreau also uses hyperbole, when he says he runs a mile.

6. Climax—The increasing importance of each successive renunciation emphasizes the importance of the final one.

B. 1. Metaphor—Killing time is suicide, self-destructive.

2. Simile—Smoke driven away is like the wicked driven away; wax melting in the fire is like the wicked perishing.

3. Irony—You would expect that the fellow who is chasing the woman would catch her, but instead, the woman catches the fellow.

4. Metonymy—Diadem (a jeweled crown) stands for the king's rule.

5. Polysyndeton—The repeated conjunctions imply the deliberate piling on of examples of where the bank's money is invested.

6. Personification—Wisdom can speak.

C. *A Christmas Carol*
   Line 1: Metaphor (hand at the grind-stone)
   Line 2: Asyndeton (squeezing, wrenching, grasping, scraping, clutching, covetous)
   Line 3: Simile (hard and sharp as a flint)
   Line 4: Simile (solitary as an oyster)
   Lines 4-6: Personification (The cold within Scrooge seems almost malicious in its activities, culminating in speaking out shrewdly in Scrooge's voice.)
   Lines 7-8: Polysyndeton (on his head and on his eyebrows and his chin)
   Lines 5-10: Metaphor (Scrooge is ice.)
   Line 12: Personification (wind was bitter)
   Line 13: Personification (snow was intent on its purpose)
   Line 14: Personification (rain was open to entreaty)
   Line 14: Personification (foul weather knows)
   Lines 12-14: Asyndeton (no wind, no falling snow, no pelting rain)
   Line 15: Polysyndeton (rain and snow and hail and sleet)
   Line 16: Personification (rain, snow, hail, sleet boast)

Lesson 16: Parallelism

I. A. Explain Parallelism
1. Tell me and I ... Teach me and I ... Involve me and I ...

2. my yoke is ... my burden is

3. to go to the house of ...to go to the house of ...

4. our Lives ... our Fortunes ...our Honor

5. reflects my ... confines my ... reinforces my

6. to temper, to cut, to polish, to become

Lesson 17: Chiasmus

I. A. Explain Chiasmus
1. sheds blood man
   man blood shed

2. day frolic
   dance night.

3. beginning end
   end beginning

4. charm strength
   strength charm

5. fair foul
   foul fair

6. often thoughts
   prayers always

7. throat parched
   glazed eye

8. eat live
   live eat

Lesson 18: Antithesis

I. A. Explain Antithesis
 1. small/giant; step/leap — This small step was a giant milestone in man's history.

 2. err/forgive; human/divine — Making mistakes comes naturally to humans; forgiving the mistakes of others does not.

 3. vices/virtues; no/few — Perhaps our vices makes it necessary for us to experience grace, and therefore, be willing to give grace to others.

 4. vice/virtue; capitalism/socialism; unequal/equal; blessings/miseries — Perhaps these two economic systems are merely two sides of the same coin.

 5. love/hate; neighbor/enemy — Jesus turns this antithesis on its head.

 6. less/more; living/die; slaves/free men — Brutus says that Rome can't have both Caesar and freedom.

Lesson 19: Anaphora

I. A. Explain Anaphora
 1. Blessed are the ... for theirs/they — Expressing this picture of Kingdom citizens with anaphora makes it more emphatic and memorable than if it had been expressed in a long and detailed explanation.

 2. I have a dream. — King's repeated phrase unifies the ideas in his speech into a single driving persuasive force.

Lesson 20: Epistrophe

I. A. Explain Epistrophe
1. as we need to be — We're up to the task!

2. good — The repeated use of the word *good* drives home the point. Take out the epistrophe and the sentence loses its impact.

3. bond — We get the message that the bond was the important thing to Shylock.

4. we are — This epistrophe communicates the stripped down belief that we are what we are.

5. the blues — This epistrophe emphasizes the cause and effect between having the blues and singing the blues.

Lesson 21: Anadiplosis

I. A. Explain Anadiplosis
1. note — Emphasizes the sound made by the bell.

2. performance; standard/sub-standard — Emphasizes the logical progression from excellent performance to sub-standard performance.

3. suffering/endurance/character/hope — Emphasizes the logical progression from suffering to hope.

4. fear/hate — Emphasizes the logical progression from fear to hate.

Lesson 22: Epanalepsis

I. A. Explain Epanalepsis
1. mankind — Crafts a memorable aspiration.

2. rejoice — Emphasizes the imperative.

3. be — Inspires.

4. king — Illustrates the succession from one king to the next.

5. horse — Underscores the king's need for a horse.

6. control — Emphasizes the importance.

Lesson 23: Review

I. Identifying Rhetorical Devices
    A. 1. Antithesis
       2. Anaphora
       3. Parallelism
       4. Epistrophe
       5. Chiasmus
       6. Anadiplosis
       7. Epanalepsis

II. Recognizing Rhetorical Devices
    A. 1. Anadiplosis (Sam), Epanalepsis (I am), Chiasmus (I Sam/Sam I)

       2. Parallelism (if..he), Antithesis (begin/end, certainty/doubt)

       3. Parallelism (feet almost stumbled/steps nearly slipped)

       4. Anadiplosis (waste of breath), Chiasmus (years waste/waste years), Antithesis (years to come/years behind)

       5. Anaphora (the more we), Epistrophe (do), (Symploce)

       6. Antithesis (first/last), Chiasmus (first last/last first)

B. 1. Hyperbole (you must hate your family to be Christ's disciple); Polysyndeton

2. Synecdoche (flesh and blood stand for the whole body)

3. Parallelism (to strive, to seek, to find, to yield); Climax (strive, seek, find); Litotes (not to yield)

4. Litotes (no minor matter)

5. Epanalepsis (believe)

6. Asyndeton

7. Allusion (manger alludes to Christ; Krypton and Jor-El allude to Superman)

C. Gettysburg Address
Lines 1,2 & 7-8: Antithesis (images of birth: brought forth, conceived / images of death: gave their lives)
Line 5: Anaphora (so)
Lines 7-8: Antithesis (gave their lives/nation might live)
Lines 9-10: Anaphora (we can not); Asyndeton; Climax (dedicate, consecrate, hallow)
Lines 9, 15: Antithesis (we cannot dedicate the ground/we can dedicate ourselves to finishing the work)
Line 10: Antithesis (living/dead)
Line 11: Antithesis (add/detract)
Line 12: Litotes (nor long remember)
Lines 12-13: Litotes (never forget)
Lines 12-13: Antithesis (won't remember/never forget); Symploce (what we say here, what they did here)
Lines 16, 18, 19: Anaphora (that); Asyndeton
Line 19: Personification (freedom is born)
Line 20: Parallelism, Epistrophe, Asyndeton (of the people, by the people, for the people)
Line 20: Litotes (not perish)

Lesson 24: Ellipsis

I. A. Explain Ellipsis
　1. get—verb

　2. ended—verb

　3. is better—verb and predicate adjective

　4. maketh—verb

　5. the man—subject

　6. I'll give—subject and verb

Lesson 25: Erotema

I. A. Explain Erotema
　1. Yes! You should buy our product.

　2. Many roads. It takes a long time to become a man.

　3. A special creation of God.

　4. No one!

　5. Never!

　6. Yes. He's the same as you.

Lesson 26: Alliteration

I. A. Identify Alliteration
   1. <u>c</u>ake, <u>k</u>ite, <u>c</u>anary

   2. <u>c</u>ity, <u>s</u>orry, <u>s</u>ister, <u>c</u>ynical

   3. <u>pn</u>eumonia, <u>kn</u>ight, <u>n</u>ight, <u>kn</u>ew, <u>mn</u>emonic

B. Identify Alliteration
   1. whisper, words, wisdom

   2. don't, drink, drive

   3. stood, still, stopped, sound, street; cry, came

   4. don't, dream, drive

   5. sessions, sweet, silent, summon, sign, sought; with, woes, wail waste

   6. wild, whirling, words

Lesson 27: Assonance

I. A. Identify Assonance
   1. l<u>a</u>ke, w<u>ei</u>ght, br<u>ai</u>d

   2. c<u>i</u>ty, n<u>i</u>bble, s<u>y</u>llable

   3. pl<u>ea</u>se, n<u>ie</u>ce, sk<u>i</u>, tr<u>ee</u>, ch<u>ea</u>p

B. Identify Assonance
1. beats, sweeps, cleans

2. flitting, still, sitting,

3. night, high, sky, lighting; rose, over, ghostly; came, bathed, day;

4. age, rave, day, rage; old, close; dying, light

5. poetry, old, goes, oldest, so, old, no, knows, poems; living, things

Lesson 28: Oxymoron

I. A. Identify Oxymoron
   1. careful disorderliness — Sometimes disorderliness is deliberate.

   2. joyful trouble — Sometimes we're happy to be inconvenienced.

   3. humbly bold — We can be bold in a humble way.

   4. miserable abundance / beggarly riches — Sometimes less is more.

   5. brawling love / loving hate / heavy lightness / serious vanity / chaos of forms / feather of lead / bright smoke / cold fire / sick health / waking sleep — Love does crazy things to us!

Lesson 29: Onomatopoeia

I. A. Identify Onomatopoeia
   scream, shriek, clamorous, clang, clash, roar, twanging, clanging, jangling, clamor, clangor

Lesson 30: Review

I. Identifying Rhetorical Devices
A. 1. Assonance
   2. Erotema
   3. Onomatopoeia
   4. Alliteration
   5. Oxymoron
   6. Ellipsis

II. Recognizing Rhetorical Devices
A. 1. Alliteration—soul, selects, society; Assonance—soul, society

   2. Assonance—mellow, wedding, bells

   3. Erotema

   4. Ellipsis—omits "The world is"

   5. Onomatopoeia—thunder; Assonance (crumbling, thunder)

   6. Oxymoron—apparent contradiction: "little big," "pretty ugly"

B. 1. Epanalepsis (brother); Chiasmus (brother friend / friend brother)

   2. Simile (a house is like a body); Alliteration (soul, sprite)

   3. Antithesis (wise/fool, enemies/friends); Ellipsis (draws advantage from); Alliteration (fool, friends); Paradox (apparent contradiction)

   4. Litotes (not niggardly); Alliteration (courtesy, counsel, countenance)

   5. Epistrophe (enough); Irony (you wouldn't expect good cyder to be in a list of such important things as bread, peace, and money.)

   6. Symploce (He / much); Paradox (apparent contradiction)

   7. Anaphora (sudden); Personification (insolent power, saucy liberty); Antithesis (sudden/gradually); Ellipsis (is apt to be)

8. Ellipsis (brings); Anaphora (nothing); Antithesis (pain/pleasure, bondage/liberty, nothing/too much); Paradox (apparent contradiction)

C. "The Raven"
   Line 1: Assonance (dreary, weak, weary)
   Line 2: Assonance (many, quaint; volume, forgotten; forgotten, lore)
   Line 3: Alliteration (nodded, nearly, napping); Onomatopoeia (tapping)
   Line 4: Onomatopoeia (rapping); Anadiplosis (rapping, rapping)
   Line 5: Onomatopoeia (muttered, tapping); Assonance ('tis, visitor)
   Line 7: Assonance (remember, bleak, December)
   Line 8: Personification (ember wrought its ghost)
   Line 9: Assonance (morrow, sought, borrow)
   Line 10: Anadiplosis (sorrow, sorrow); Assonance (sorrow, lost); Alliteration (lost Lenore)
   Line 11: Alliteration (rare, radiant); Assonance (rare, radiant, maiden, name)
   Line 13: Asyndeton (silken, sad, uncertain); Alliteration (silken, sad, certain); Assonance (uncertain, purple, curtain); Onomatopoeia (rustling)
   Line 14: Epistrophe (me); Oxymoron (fantastic terrors); Assonance (terrors, never, felt, before)
   Line 16: Assonance ('tis, visitor); Alliteration (entreating, entrance)